POWER
Prayers
to Start Your Day

DONNA K. MALTESE

BARBOUR
PUBLISHING

Dedication

To my children, Jen and Zach, who have taught me so much about this journey we call life. To Mom, Di, and Jo for always being there, through thick and thin. To Pastor Geib and the Silverdale Church for their constant love and prayers. To Connie Troyer of Barbour Publishing for her unflagging encouragement and faith in me. To my husband, Pete—the love of my life—without whom this book would not have been possible.

Member of the
Evangelical Christian
Publishers Association

Contents

Introduction

Every new morning is spread before us like a blank canvas to paint as we choose. And the beginning of each new morning provides us with a choice as to who will be guiding our brush that day. Will it be our egocentric selves or our loving God? If we are wise, we will allow our hand to be directed by the Master Painter, the Ultimate Designer. He is our Creator, Companion, Protector, Confidant, and Friend, the One that can help us face whatever life may bring. Only in His power can we push away feelings of doubt, disappointment, dismay, and discouragement and fill our minds with hope, joy, peace, creativity, and a sense of expectancy. *Power Prayers to Start Your Day* promises to aid in this early morning quest to seek God—for guidance, comfort, instruction, direction, strength, and love.

No less a Bible figure than King David recognized the importance of prayer and guidance at the start of the day. He cried, "Let the morning bring me word of your unfailing love, for I have put my trust in you. Show me the way I should go, for to you I lift up my soul" (Psalm 143:8 NIV).

Jesus Himself made prayer an "a.m." priority. The verses prior to Mark 1:35 describe one of the most hectic days of Jesus' life, a day in which He had worked from sunrise to sundown, preaching, healing, teaching, performing miracles, settling disputes, and so on. And the morning following that most hectic day was the morning that Jesus *chose* to get up "very early in the morning, while it was still dark" and go "off to a solitary place, where he prayed" (Mark 1:35 NIV). Do you *choose* to be *that* committed to prayer?

If we who claim "to live in him [are to] walk as Jesus did" (1 John 2:6 NIV), it seems clear that, no matter how weary we are, once the sand has been rubbed out of our eyes, our minds should be reaching for God as we seek His will for us that day. According to E. M. Bounds, author of *Power through Prayer*, "The men who have done the most for God in this world have been early on their knees. He who fritters away the early morning, its opportunity and freshness, in other pursuits than seeking God will make poor headway seeking him the rest of the day. If God is not first in our thoughts and efforts in the morning, he will be in the last place the remainder of the day."[1]

In the morning we need to enter our place of prayer, close the door, and meet with God to receive our marching orders. This time with God is our morning manna, our breakfast feast on Christ. In Exodus 16:15–16, Moses said to the children of Israel, "[Manna] is the bread the Lord has given you to eat. This is what the Lord has commanded: 'Each one is to gather as much as he needs' " (NIV). Regarding this scripture, Matthew Henry comments, "Christ himself is the true manna, the bread of life. . . . We must every one of us gather [manna] for ourselves, and gather in the morning of our days, the morning of our opportunities, which if we let slip, it may be too late to gather."[2]

Once we have gathered our supernatural provision of morning manna, once we have feasted upon Christ and the Word, we can then rise in His strength to face the challenges of the day.

St. Patrick, the renowned missionary to Ireland in the fifth century, is credited with writing the following "rising" prayer, portions of which appear below:

Breastplate of St. Patrick

I arise today, through
God's strength to pilot me,
God's might to uphold me,
God's wisdom to guide me,
God's eye to look before me,
God's ear to hear me,
God's word to speak to me,
God's hand to guard me,
God's way to lie before me,
God's shield to protect me,
God's host to save me. . . .
Christ with me,

Christ before me,
Christ behind me,
Christ in me,
Christ beneath me,
Christ above me,
Christ on my right,
Christ on my left,
Christ when I lie down,
Christ when I sit down,
Christ when I arise,
Christ in the heart of every [one] who thinks of me,
Christ in the mouth of every one who speaks of me,
Christ in the eye of every one that sees me,
Christ in every ear that hears me.[3]

What strength there is in rising! Saint Patrick was a man longing for God's presence every waking moment. He was a man who, upon rising, sought God's face and will for his life. With his breastplate of prayer, Saint Patrick armed himself to face the Goliaths of his day and, as a result, did mighty deeds for God. He spent his life traveling throughout Ireland, preaching, teaching, building churches, opening schools, and performing miracles.

Are you hungry for morning manna? Do you desire more of God's presence and power in your life? Are you armed to face the challenges of the day? Allow *Power Prayers to Start Your Day* to help you in your quest to pursue God. In doing so, may the Spirit increase your faith and power, stirring you to truly believe Jesus' promise: "Anyone who has faith in me will do what I have been doing. He will do even greater things than these" (John 14:12 NIV).

How to Use This Book

Power Prayers to Start Your Day can be the springboard to your private early morning prayer time with God. Each chapter contains a brief introduction of a topic, such as your quiet time, faith, relationships, work, and health. At the end of each chapter introduction, you will find a portion of Saint Patrick's "rising prayer," reminding you to keep Christ close to you as you meet the challenges of each day. This is followed by fourteen prayers to provide a starting point for your own prayers.

Read the words aloud as you pray and then add whatever the Spirit puts upon your heart. Remember that prayer is simply a way of communicating with our Friend and Savior, Jesus Christ. He is ready to take your hand and lead you to Father God. And no matter what we pray, our words need not be perfect. For "the Spirit helps us in our weakness. . . . The Spirit himself intercedes for us with groans that words cannot express" (Romans 8:26 NIV).

Finally, remember that prayer is a two-way street. After you've spent some time praying, be sure to spend time in silence before God, listening for His direction—His instructions for your day.

The best way to make morning prayer part of your daily routine is to *begin*. Start gathering your manna in bite-sized pieces, beginning with five minutes of prayer each morning. Then gradually increase your manna intake as the Lord leads you.

As you continue to seek God every morning, Jesus will come and touch you, saying, " 'Arise, and do not be afraid' " (Matthew 17:7 NKJV).

> *Finally, be strong in the Lord and in his mighty*
>
> *power. . . . And pray in the Spirit on all occasions*
>
> *with all kinds of prayers and requests.*
>
> EPHESIANS 6:10, 18 NIV

The Power of Stillness Before God

This is what the Sovereign LORD, the Holy One of Israel, says...
"In quietness and trust is your strength."
ISAIAH 30:15 NIV

*I*n this fast-paced, noisy world, quiet time is a precious commodity. If cell phones aren't ringing, the dog is barking or the kids are arguing. If the television isn't on, a CD player is blaring nearby. If people aren't talking, your computer is telling you that "You've got mail!" That's why the early morning hours are ideal for quiet time before the Lord. The morning is your chance to spend time with God before the world fully awakens.

To ready your heart and mind for a meaningful time of prayer, adopt the three habits recommended by David Jeremiah. First, *anticipate* His presence. God is coming to see you, His sole desire to spend precious moments with you. Second, *acknowledge* that God is now present, sitting in the chair beside you, ready to listen to your petitions and give you advice and direction. Finally, *acclimate* your mind, body, and heart to receive and accept His Word and direction.[4]

When your heart, mind, and body have been readied, call upon the Holy Spirit to help you pray. Rachel Hickson, author of *Supernatural Communication*, says the Holy Spirit is "like an 'adapter' that helps us align correctly to our heavenly power source. . . . [Prayer] is not just about you; it is about your prayer being connected to the transformer of the Holy Spirit. Now your prayer can be powerful. . . . Whatever else you use to help you get into the place of prayer are wonderful, but it is actually *this connection* that is going to transform your prayer life."[5]

So, as the Glade commercial says about the air freshener, "Plug it in, plug it in." Find your peace and then plug in to the Holy Spirit. Once you connect, the power of your prayers will be awesome, allowing you to be strengthened by the Pilot of your life as you pray for yourself, others, and the world.

Once you've told Him everything that's on your mind, make sure you spend some time *listening*. Open your ears and your heart to what God has to say. Neil Anderson writes, "Prayer is personal and two-way. You have entered into a new dimension of spirituality when you are comfortable in His presence and don't feel obligated to talk. . . . Those who learn to 'practice His presence' have learned to 'pray without ceasing' (1 Thessalonians 5:17). . . . When I leave my quiet times, I leave with God—and prayer doesn't stop!"[6]

God is ever ready to help us seek peace and quiet in this hectic world. So enter that quiet place, remembering that when you pray, He will listen (see Jeremiah 29:12). Once you've said "Amen," remain silent and listen, for God is also ready to speak and to guide you through this life. "I will instruct you and teach you in the way you should go" (Psalm 32:8 NIV). Amid His presence you will receive His courage and strength to meet the day. What a wonderful God we have!

I arise today, through God's strength to pilot me.

Waiting on the Lord

*Wait on the LORD; be of good courage, and He shall
strengthen your heart; wait, I say, on the LORD!*
PSALM 27:14 NKJV

*D*ear Lord, as I enter into this quiet time with You, calm my
mind, body, and spirit. Take my hand and lead me to Your
side. I long to feel Your touch, hear Your voice, and see Your
face. Whatever comes to me this day, I know You will be with
me, as You are now—within me, above me, beside me. Thank
You for strengthening my heart. Thank You for giving me the
patience to wait on You.

Quiet Waters

He makes me lie down in green pastures, he leads me beside quiet waters.
PSALM 23:2 NIV

*M*y Shepherd, my Lord, my Savior, lead me beside the still
waters. Lie with me in the green pastures. Restore my soul.
Lead me down the paths of Your choosing today. With You
by my side, I fear no evil. You are my Comfort and my Guide.
I am happy in Your presence. Your goodness and Your mercy
are with me this minute, this hour, and this day. Thank You,
Lord, for leading me here and making me whole—for being
the Shepherd of my life.

Morning Meditation

Give heed to the voice of my cry, my King and my God, for to you I will pray. My voice You shall hear in the morning, O LORD; in the morning I will direct it to You, and I will look up. . . . Make Your way straight before my face.

PSALM 5:2–3, 8 NKJV

*Y*ou defend me, You love me, You lead me. How great is that! How great are You! Too wonderful for words. This morning in Your presence, I rejoice. This morning, I direct my prayers to You, knowing that You will hear my words and interpret my groans. I am directing my voice to You, Lord, and patiently await Your instructions.

Strength in God

May honor and thanks be given to the Lord, because He has heard my prayer. The Lord is my strength and my safe cover. My heart trusts in Him, and I am helped.

PSALM 28:6–7 NLV

*L*ord, I know You hear my voice when I pray to You! You are my strength and my shield. When my heart trusts in You, I am overjoyed. You give me courage to meet the challenges of the day. You give me strength to do the tasks You have set before me. You build me up, raise me to the heights, and lead me to places I would never have dreamed were possible. You are the Friend who will never leave me, the Guide who walks before me. With You in my life, I can do anything.

Living Water

Early the next morning. . .she went on her way and wandered in the desert. . . .
Then God opened her eyes and she saw a well of water.
GENESIS 21:14, 19 NIV

*L*ord, thank You for being with me as I spend my quiet time in Your presence. When I am in the wilderness, You tell me not to fear. You tell me to rise in Your strength. And then You open my eyes and direct me to the living water. Lord, there is no one like You, no one who loves me as You do. I thirst for Your presence and am rewarded with Your peace. Be Thou my eternal fount of blessing.

Renewal of Strength

Those who hope in the LORD will renew their strength. They will soar on wings like
eagles; they will run and not grow weary, they will walk and not be faint.
ISAIAH 40:31 NIV

*L*ord, I come to You in this early morning time, my heart at peace, my mouth at rest. As I wait upon You, You come to me, eager to talk and to listen. As I spend time here with You, my strength is renewed. I mount up with wings like eagles. With You by my side, I can run and not be weary, walk and not be faint. Be with me here and now, today and forever.

Peace Like a River

"I am the Lord your God, Who teaches you to do well, Who leads you in the way you should go. If only you had listened to My Laws! Then your peace would have been like a river and your right-standing with God would have been like the waves of the sea."
ISAIAH 48:17–18 NLV

*L*ord, my Pilot and my Guide, give me direction this day. You teach me what is best for me and direct me in the way I should go. When I pay attention to Your commands, You give me peace like a river. It is to Your living water that I run. Help me, Lord, to obey You in all I say and do. Give me the wisdom to abide in Your Word, all to Your glory!

Morning Sustenance

The Sovereign LORD has given me an instructed tongue, to know the word that sustains the weary. He wakens me morning by morning, wakens my ear to listen like one being taught.
ISAIAH 50:4 NIV

*L*ord, although I am tired this morning, You will give me all the strength I need to meet the challenges of the day. Your Word sustains me when I am weary. You awaken me morning by morning. I am ready, Lord, to listen to Your voice. Teach me what You would have me learn today. My only desire is to bring glory to Your name, Lord. May everything I do today be pleasing in Your sight.

Rejoice!

This is the day which the LORD hath made; we will rejoice and be glad in it.
PSALM 118:24 KJV

*T*his is the day that You have made, Lord! I will rejoice and be glad in it! Lord, I feel Your light shining upon me. I feel Your presence all around me. I glory in Your touch! No matter what comes against me today, I know that You will be with me, so there is no reason to be afraid. All I have to do is reach for You and You are here with me. You are so good to me. Thank You, Lord, for Your goodness and Your love.

God of Peace

For God is not a God of disorder but of peace.
1 CORINTHIANS 14:33 NIV

*G*od, sometimes life is so messy. Nothing has been going right. All I want to do is throw up my hands in frustration. But that is not of You, Lord. You are not a God of disorder but a God of peace. Help me, Lord, to be at peace now as I come to You in prayer. Help me to rest in Your presence and gain Your strength to meet the challenges of this day.

Strength for the Day

O LORD, be gracious to us; we have waited for You. Be their
strength every morning, our salvation also in the time of distress.
ISAIAH 33:2 NASB

*O*h God, I long for Your presence and Your touch. Deliver me from worry, fear, and distress. Bind me with Your love and forgiveness as I rest in You. Fill me with Your power and Your strength to meet the challenges of this day. Thank You, Lord, for the way You are working in my life. Keep me close to You throughout this day.

Resting in His Arms

[Jesus] said to them, "Come away by yourselves
to a secluded place and rest a while."
MARK 6:31 NASB

*L*ord, it seems that these days I can't get enough rest. I seem to be always on the run. Calm my heart and my soul. Bathe my thoughts in Your light. I come seeking Your peace, resting in Your arms. Within this early morning silence, speak to me. Tell me what You would have me do this day. And when I come to You as night falls, lead me back to Your Word and then give me the rest I need.

No Worries

"Peace I leave with you. My peace I give to you. I do not give peace to you as the world gives. Do not let your hearts be troubled or afraid."
JOHN 14:27 NLV

*L*ord, it's hard to find peace in this world. Help me not to be distracted by the noise without and within. Once I come to You, within the stillness of these early morning hours, my thoughts, heart, and spirit will be at rest. When I find You and abide within You, I have no worries, no troubles, no fears. Ah. . .You are peace. You are life. You are the way.

Filled with Manna

May the God of hope fill you with all joy and peace as you trust in him, so that you may overflow with hope by the power of the Holy Spirit.
ROMANS 15:13 NIV

*J*esus, oh Jesus, I come to You as an empty vessel, waiting and wanting to be filled with Your joy and peace. As I trust in You to see me through this day, I am filled with hope. I expect good things to happen today as You empower me. For no matter what happens, I have Your love, forgiveness, and bounty with me always.

The Power of Belief

"Everything is possible for him who believes."
MARK 9:23 NIV

A man brought his demon-possessed son to Jesus and said, " 'If you can do anything, take pity on us and help us' " (Mark 9:22 NIV). Jesus' response is a seemingly incredulous " '*If* you can'?" [emphasis added], followed by the simple yet mind-boggling statement, " 'Everything is possible for him who believes' " (Mark 9:23 NIV). We can imagine that the boy's father was immediately torn between hope and despair, wanting to believe Jesus yet unable to deny the reality before him. Mark records the father's desperate response: " 'I do believe; help me overcome my unbelief!' " (9:23 NIV).

Do you sometimes feel like the father of this boy? One moment you're telling Jesus, "I believe, Lord, I believe," and then ten seconds later you're tearing yourself apart, thinking, *Well, I think I believe. . .but maybe I don't?*

Remember when the disciples saw Jesus walking on the water toward them? They thought He was a ghost and cried out in *fear.*

> *But Jesus immediately said to them: "Take courage! It is I. Don't be afraid." "Lord, if it's you," Peter replied, "tell me to come to you on the water." "Come," he said. Then Peter got out of the boat,*

walked on the water and came toward Jesus.
But when he saw the wind, he was afraid and,
beginning to sink, cried out, "Lord, save me!"
Immediately Jesus reached out his hand and caught
him. "You of little faith," he said, "why did you
doubt?"

MATTHEW 14:27–31 NIV

Before this event occurred, Peter had already seen Jesus heal a leper, mute demoniacs, his own mother-in-law, and more. He'd even been present when Jesus demonstrated His power over nature by calming the wind. Still, after witnessing all these miracles, Peter wavered on the water. Why? E. M. Bounds provides this answer: "Doubt and fear are the twin foes of faith."[7]

Knowing this disciple would eventually sink, why did Jesus invite him out of the boat? Matthew Henry writes, "Christ bid [Peter to] come, not only that he might walk upon the water, and so know Christ's power, but that he might sink, and so know his own weakness."[8]

Knowing that even Peter doubted at times provides us with a little relief. Again, Matthew Henry writes: "The strongest faith and the greatest courage have a mixture of fear. Those that can say, *Lord, I believe*, must say, *Lord, help my unbelief*."[9]

Like Peter, when we begin to panic and find ourselves sinking, we must cry out in specific and fervent prayer to Jesus, saying, "Lord, save me!" And as Jesus did with Peter, He will *immediately* reach out and save us.

By keeping our eyes off our difficulties and fixed on Jesus, we will overcome our doubts and fears and find ourselves walking on the living water of His power, His Word, and His promises. We must be unwavering in our faith that God will uphold us no matter what our trial.

Each morning, arm yourself before you step out of your

boat. To keep your heart from wavering, plant these words in your heart: " 'Everything is possible for him who believes' " (Mark 9:23 NIV). Then as you pray in faith and in accordance with His will, do not doubt in your heart but believe you will have what you ask. Because Jesus promises that indeed you *will* have it! He *will* answer your prayers. He will not let you sink in the sea of doubt, fear, and despair! Just keep your eyes on Jesus and your heart in the Word, and God, in His strength, will keep you walking on the waters of great expectations.

I arise today, through. . .
God's might to uphold me.

Feeding on Faithfulness

Trust in the LORD, and do good; dwell in the land,
and feed on His faithfulness.

PSALM 37:3 NKJV

*A*s I dwell on this earth and take in my early morning manna, I feel Your presence beside me. I remember the times You've taken care of me, suffered with me, and led me through the darkness, and I feed on these memories. I feed on Your faithfulness. Thank You for always being there for me. Remain with me now and for the rest of this day, giving me courage and strength as I trust in You.

Access to Peace and Grace

Therefore, having been justified by faith, we have peace with God through
our Lord Jesus Christ, through whom also we have access by faith into
this grace in which we stand, and rejoice in hope of the glory of God.

ROMANS 5:1–2 NKJV

*I*t is my faith in You, Jesus, that keeps me sane and gives me peace. I am eternally grateful for that peace, and I thank You. My faith in You justifies me and gives me the grace I need to forgive others. Help me to do that today. Help me to look at those who have wounded me as You look at me—without blame and with love. Keep me in Your hand and give me Your strength as I go through this day.

Unwavering Faith

*Yet [Abraham] did not waver through unbelief regarding the
promise of God, but was strengthened in his faith and gave glory to God,
being fully persuaded that God had power to do what he had promised.*
ROMANS 4:20–21 NIV

*L*ord, let me be like Abraham, with unwavering faith and belief
in Your promises. May I be strengthened by Your Word as I
meditate on it before You today, knowing and believing that
You have the power to do what You have promised. I believe
that You will be with me forever, that You will never leave me
nor forsake me, that You will keep my head above the water,
and that You love me now and to the end of my days. Thank
You, Lord, for saving my soul and strengthening my faith.

Standing Firm

Watch, stand fast in the faith, be brave, be strong.
1 CORINTHIANS 16:13 NKJV

*G*od, I don't feel very strong today. In fact, I am filled with
that sinking-like-Peter feeling. Buoy my faith, Lord, so that
I can stand firm. As I meditate on how You stopped the wind
and calmed the sea, how just a touch of Your hand healed
others, how there was power even in the hem of Your garment,
I know I can stand today, firm in You. Continue filling me
with Your power, courage, and strength.

Living Water

Our life is lived by faith. We do not live by what we see in front of us.
2 CORINTHIANS 5:7 NLV

*O*h God, I see the waves crashing around me, my troubles overwhelming me. I feel as if I am sinking with no foothold to save me! Come to me, Lord. Cover me with Your love. Lord, I believe! Help my unbelief! I refuse to look at all the troubles around me. I will keep my eyes on You only. I see Your light and love, Your precious face, Your lips telling me, "It is I; do not be afraid. Just believe." I believe, Lord! I believe!

Strengthened in the Faith

Just as you received Christ Jesus as Lord, continue to live in him,
rooted and built up in him, strengthened in the faith as you were taught,
and overflowing with thankfulness.
COLOSSIANS 2:6–7 NIV

*J*esus, my Jesus, thank You for always being with me, holding me up above the waters of this life, especially when the current is more than I can bear. As You uphold me, day by day, morning by morning, my faith grows. There is no one like You, Jesus. No one like You. I am strengthened during this time with You. I overflow with thankfulness and praise. What would I ever do without You in my life?

Open Eyes, Endless Hope

I pray that the eyes of your heart may be enlightened, so that you will know what is the hope of His calling, what are the riches of the glory of His inheritance in the saints, and what is the surpassing greatness of His power toward us who believe.
EPHESIANS 1:18–19 NASB

*E*ach morning You open the eyes of my heart and fill me with Your awesome resurrection power. As I seek Your face, I am filled with endless hope. I revel in Your glorious riches. I am saved by the power of belief. Enlighten my mind, heart, and spirit as we spend these moments together. I await Your words, dear Lord. Speak to me now!

The Joy of Belief

Though you have not seen Him, you love him, and though you do not see Him now, but believe in Him, you greatly rejoice with joy inexpressible and full of glory.
1 PETER 1:8 NASB

*W*hat incredible joy fills my soul! I love You, Lord, and am filled with Your love for me. Words cannot express the glorious joy I feel at this moment, basking in Your morning light, warmed by Your presence at my side. I want You to be with me throughout this entire day. Never leave me. Never forsake me. Give me that faith that believes in things unseen!

Firmly Anchored

If any of you lack wisdom, let him ask of God. . . . But let him ask in faith,
nothing wavering. For he that wavereth is like a wave of the
sea driven with the wind and tossed.

JAMES 1:5–6 KJV

*L*ord, I read in Your Word about the miracles that You have performed. I have seen such miracles in my own life. Help me not to give in to that sinking-like-Peter feeling, one full of doubt. Help me not to be blown and tossed by the wind but firmly anchored in the harbor of Your Word, Your love, and Your promises.

No Doubt about It

"Have faith in God. . . . For assuredly, I say to you, whoever. . .does not doubt in his
heart, but believes that those things he says will be done, he will have whatever he says."

MARK 11:22–23 NKJV

*H*oly Spirit, it all comes down to faith in God. Fill my heart with assurance, with confidence, and with the promise from Jesus that everything is possible for him who believes. Clear my mind, soul, and spirit of any lingering doubts, even those that I have hidden. Allow me to rest in the confidence and belief in my Savior.

Rewards of Belief

But without faith it is impossible to please him: for he that cometh to God
must believe that he is, and that he is a rewarder of them that diligently seek him.
HEBREWS 11:6 KJV

*F*rom the beginning of time, Lord, You have been the One. You are the Ancient of Days. I humbly come before You, earnestly seeking Your face. I am awed by Your presence and staggered by Your might and power. Hear my prayer, O Lord. Reward me with Your peace and Your strength. I believe in You.

Fixing Our Eyes on Jesus

Let us fix our eyes on Jesus, the author and perfecter of our faith.
HEBREWS 12:2 NIV

*J*esus, I am not looking at the waves surrounding me. I am ignoring the wind that makes the sea restless. I am fixing my eyes on You as I step out of the boat and walk to You. Nothing can frighten me, nothing can move me. You are my salvation. I'm running to You! I am safe in Your arms!

Hopeful Surety

Now faith is the substance of things hoped for,
the evidence of things not seen.
HEBREWS 11:1 KJV

*A*lthough I cannot see or touch You, Lord, You are here with me. You are waiting to hear my prayer, ready to do what's best for me. You know me better than I know myself. Thank You for spending these precious moments here with me as I open my heart and share my hopes, dreams, fears, and needs with You. Increase my faith as I hope in You.

Faith and Wellness

"Rise and go; your faith has made you well."
LUKE 17:19 NIV

*N*ine simple words—*"Rise and go; your faith has made you well."* What a treasure they are! Keep them in my mind and heart today. Help me to retain their sounds, meaning, and import. May I rise from this place of prayer full of faith that heals my mind, body, spirit, and soul. Thank You, Lord.

The Power of Creative Vision

Be careful how you live, not as fools but as those who are wise.
Make the most of every opportunity.
EPHESIANS 5:15–16 NLT

*T*he word *opportunity* is derived from the Latin nautical term, *opportunus*, which denoted "favorable winds." Because such winds were advantageous to ships seeking harbor, *opportunus* came to mean "coming at a convenient time."[10]

Many people look back upon their lives as a series of missed opportunities. Are you one of them?

We cannot change the past, nor can we waste the present by lamenting over how many times we've allowed the winds of opportunity to pass us by. Don't let yourself become mired in the "would've-could've-should've" mode. Take the following steps to ensure that you make the most of every opportunity in the future.

First, *pray for creative vision.* Take your ideas to Jesus, the One by whom "all things were created. . .visible and invisible" (Colossians 1:16 NKJV). In *Living and Praying in Jesus' Name*, Dick Eastman and Jack Hayford explain: "In Jesus' name we can pray for Christ's creative power to flow into every situation we encounter. His name truly creates. Creativity is defined as 'the combining of two separate ideas to form a totally new idea.' Therefore, when we pray in Jesus' name and present our ideas to Christ, He combines them with His creative genius, which results in the birth of altogether new ideas."[11] Jesus is just waiting for you to prayerfully present your thoughts, dreams, and ideas to Him.

Second, *listen expectantly.* After you have prayed for creative vision, be still, open your mind, and *expect* God to speak to you. In the book of James we read, "If you need wisdom—if you want to know what God wants you to do—ask him, and he will gladly tell you. . . . But when you ask him, *be sure that you really expect him to answer*, for a doubtful mind is as unsettled as a wave of the sea that is driven and tossed by the wind" (James 1:5–6 NLT, emphasis added). God shares your dreams *with* you. He is eager to project His vision for you on the plasma screen of your expectant mind. And once you have that vision, He is waiting to open up a new world of possibilities.

Third, begin to *pay attention* to what is around you. John Maxwell writes, "What are inventors? People who see opportunity in things where others see nothing—people whose senses are alive to creative possibilities. Inventors fail many times yet realize the longer they work, the more they study and the closer they look, the greater their chances for success."[12] Keep your eyes open to the "creative possibilities" surrounding you!

Fourth, *be resourceful.* Sometimes, when God is calling us into a certain area, we need to *make* our own opportunities. During these times, we would be wise to employ the maxim of comedian Milton Berle: "If opportunity doesn't knock, build a door." After building your door, other opportunities will arise and you'll find yourself continuing toward your goal—but taking a different route to get there.

And last, *have courage.* American jurist and politician James F. Byrnes said, "Too many people are thinking of security, instead of opportunity. They seem more afraid of life than death." Sometimes it seems easier to stay anchored in the place where we feel the most comfortable. But that place may not be where God wants us to be (see Deuteronomy 1:6–7 NIV). Courage is needed to set sail into unknown waters.

When God called me to the Christian publishing field, I prayed for several years for direction, all the while looking for the right opportunity. Although my part-time job as a church secretary didn't pay a lot, I was in a sheltered work environment with my pastor as my boss, and I felt blessed in my workplace. But God gave me a new creative vision. I began to see myself no longer as a church secretary but as a writer and editor for Christian publishers. So at God's insistence, and with much encouragement from my husband, I set sail for new waters. Do you have the same courage to take advantage of the opportunities God sets before you?

Don't let your ship of life rot in dry dock. *Pray* for creative vision, expect God to speak to you, pay attention to the winds blowing around you, be resourceful, and then courageously set sail, confident that God has given you the ability and gifts to take advantage of every opportunity He affords you. Through it all, remember that you are never alone: God and His creative wisdom will be with you throughout your voyage, steering you through every ocean of life!

> *I arise today, through. . .*
> *God's wisdom to guide me.*

Walking in God's Wisdom

Listen, my son, and accept what I say, and the years of your life will be many.
I guide you in the way of wisdom and lead you along straight paths. When you walk,
your steps will not be hampered; when you run, you will not stumble.
Hold on to instruction, do not let it go; guard it well, for it is your life.
PROVERBS 4:10–13 NIV

*L*ord, I want to do what You have created me to do. I come to You today, seeking Your direction for my life. I have my own ideas of how You want me to serve You, to enlarge Your kingdom here on earth, to provide for myself, my family, and my church. But I need Your wisdom. Which route should I take? When shall I begin? How shall I go? Lead me, Lord, into the waters You have chartered for my life.

Wisdom of Creation

By wisdom the LORD laid the earth's foundations, by understanding he set the heavens
in place; by his knowledge the deeps were divided, and the clouds let drop the dew.
PROVERBS 3:19–20 NIV

*G*od, Your creation is so awesome. Everywhere I look, I see Your handiwork. You have made it all. You have made me. Continue to mold me and shape me into the person You want me to be. Give me knowledge and wisdom in how best to serve You.

Master of Creation

In the beginning was the Word. . . . All things were made by him;
and without him was not any thing made that was made.
JOHN 1:1, 3 KJV

*J*esus, Jesus, Jesus. I am still this morning, before You, waiting to seek Your face, Your direction, Your wisdom, Your ideas for my life. You are the master of creation. You are in me, with me, above me, below me. You have made me. Now make of my life what You will.

Asked to Be Cocreators

And out of the ground the LORD God formed every beast of the field, and every fowl of the
air; and brought them unto Adam to see what he would call them: and whatsoever Adam
called every living creature, that was the name thereof.
GENESIS 2:19 KJV

*L*ord, You formed all things. And afterward, You invited man to be Your cocreator, allowing him to name things, do things, and serve You. Show me now, Lord, how You want me to employ my talents, my gifts, and myself to make this world a better place. Come to me now, Lord. Imprint upon my mind what You want me to do, which door You want me to walk through.

Faith in the Invisible

*By faith we understand that the worlds were prepared by the word of God,
so that what is seen was not made out of things which are visible.*

HEBREWS 11:3 NASB

I cannot see my future, Lord. I must trust in Your wisdom to guide me through these unchartered waters. Although I cannot see what the future holds, You see it, Lord. You have it all planned out. Open my ears to Your voice and my eyes to Your creative vision for my life. Help me to see where You want me to go. Then give me the courage to steer my life in that direction.

The Breath of Life

*The LORD God formed man of the dust of the ground, and breathed
into his nostrils the breath of life; and man became a living soul.*

GENESIS 2:7 KJV

*I*t is through You that I have life. Each and every day, You breathe life into my soul. You send my spirit soaring into unknown heights. Thank You for the gift of life. I dedicate it to Your service. Where would You like me to go? What shall I do? Which path shall I take? Speak to me as I remain still, listening for Your voice, awaiting Your direction.

The Right Focus

We do not know what to do, but our eyes are upon You.
2 CHRONICLES 20:12 AMP

*H*elp me, Lord, to focus on You in all I say and do, in every decision I make, and in every direction I take. Help me to make the most of each opportunity. My life's aim is to serve, obey, and seek You. I do not know what to do, but my eyes, Lord, are upon Your heavenly face, and in this I rejoice!

Advancing for God

The LORD our God said to us at Horeb, "You have stayed long enough at this mountain. Break camp and advance. . . .
See, I have given you this land. Go in and take possession. . . ."
DEUTERONOMY 1:6–8 NIV

*Y*ou have given me direction. It is time for me to move forward, to sail into unknown waters. You have commanded me to advance. You have already given me the land beyond these seas. All I need to do is sail toward You and take possession of the blessings You have provided. Thank You, God, for allowing me to be a part of Your master plan.

You Made Me!

Thy hands have made me and fashioned me.
PSALM 119:73 KJV

*Y*ou have known me since the beginning. You know my doubts and fears, yet You love me still. Sometimes I feel as if I am adrift in confusion. I need You to lovingly urge me on past that darkness and into Your light. Thank You for Your patience. Help me to create a life with You; help me to be not just a lump of clay sitting on a shelf, out of harm's way but unused. Continue to shape me and mold me into the person You want me to be.

Set Apart and Appointed

"Before I formed you in the womb I knew you, before you were born I set you apart; I appointed you."
JEREMIAH 1:5 NIV

*O*h God, before I was even conceived, You knew me and loved me. You have set me apart for a special purpose, for a way to achieve Your ends. I am nothing without You, yet You ask me to be a part of the grand plan. Even knowing my weaknesses, You have loved me. Give me the vision You have for my life so that I may best know how to serve You. Here I am, Lord. Use me!

Never Say Can't

The LORD said to me, "Do not say 'I am only a child.' You must go to everyone I send you to and say whatever I command you. Do not be afraid of them, for I am with you and will rescue you," declares the LORD.
JEREMIAH 1:7–8 NIV

I know what You want me to do, Lord. I hear Your voice telling me how You want me to serve. Help me to put aside my doubts, misgivings, and fears. I want to go where You command. I know You will be by my side through it all.

For with God, I Can!

With your help I can advance against a troop; with my God I can scale a wall.
PSALM 18:29 NIV

*W*ith You, my awesome God, all things are possible. I can do anything through You. I can climb that mountain, take that job, or whatever You are calling me to do! Like Joshua, I can be strong and courageous. No one can stand against me because You are by my side.

No Fear

This is what the LORD says — he who made you, who formed
you in the womb, and who will help you: Do not be afraid.
ISAIAH 44:2 NIV

*Y*ou've made me the way I am for a reason, for a purpose. You are the Author and the Finisher of my faith. For now and always You are there to help me. I am not afraid when my hand is in Yours. Thank You for leading me out of the darkness and into the light of Your Word.

Opportunity Knocks

And who knows but that you have come to the kingdom
for such a time as this and for this very occasion?
ESTHER 4:14 AMP

*L*ike Esther, I have been brought to this place in my life for such a time as this. I expectantly wait to hear from You, to see You, to serve You. Thank You for this opportunity to make a difference in this world and to show others how awesome You are. Direct me on the path of Your choosing. My feet are waiting to follow Your command.

My Future

The Power of Divine Guidance

For the LORD will go before you.
ISAIAH 52:12 NIV

When I was a child struggling with my future, my grandmother gave me the "gift" of a worry stone. Holding this flat, oval-shaped, polished gemstone between her fingers and thumb, Grandma showed me how to rub the stone. She said that when I did this, I would gain relief from the concerns that plagued me.

As I grew, I used this worry stone when plagued by what-ifs. "What if I flunk this exam?" *Rub, rub. . .* I got a B. "What if Daddy should die?" *Rub, rub. . .* My father died on my sixteenth birthday. "What if Mark breaks up with me?" *Rub, rub. . . I* broke up with Mark.

As the years went by, I began to realize that it didn't matter how much I used the worry stone, because it changed neither the present nor the future. So I put the stone away. . .but kept the worries close at hand.

Then, years later, I visited the only church we have in Silverdale, Pennsylvania. And there, for the first time in my life, I connected with God in a personal, life-changing way. I began attending church and Sunday school every week and diving into God's Word with an unquenchable thirst.

As I read I discovered the powerful words of Jeremiah 29:11–12: " 'For I know the plans I have for you,' declares the LORD, 'plans to prosper you and not to harm you, plans to give you hope and a future. Then you will call upon me and come and pray to me, and I will listen to you' " (NIV).

I was awestruck. God had plans for me! Plans to prosper and not to harm me! Plans to give me hope and a future! I began to revel in this knowledge. I realized that when worries began to come upon me, all I had to do was call upon Him, seek Him with all my heart, and tell Him all my fears of the future. He would listen and then lead me to go in the power of His divine guidance, urging me to be confident that He is before me in the going. He's got a plan for my life, full of hope in and prosperity with Him, and He will give me the power to proceed!

As I looked back on my past, I realized my dad's death had not been some sort of awful punishment for the sins of my life but a part of God's ultimate *plan* for my life. God intends for everything that happens to us—the good and the bad—to further His purposes for the ultimate good (see Genesis 50:19–20). And although I'd lost my earthly father, I would never lose my heavenly Father. He will always carry me through my days.

Oh, if only Grandma had given me the gift of scripture instead of a worry stone! How much easier it would have been to cope with my fears of the future and my sense of trouble in the present. How many years I wasted in the pit of despair over what-ifs, girded only with the tool of a worry stone instead of God's Word.

Becky Tirabassi writes, "When you neglect to read the Bible, you are purposefully cutting yourself off from being encouraged by [God's] voice or receiving very important and specific directions for the day, week, month, and beyond. . . .

God loves to communicate with us. He wants us to tune our hearts to Him so that in a crowded room of opinions and temptations, there is just one voice we recognize and walk toward."[13]

When worries about the future plague you, delve into God's Word, turn your heart to seek His face, and pray to the Lord your Savior who never ceases to "instruct you and teach you in the way you should go" and "guide you with [His] eye" (Psalm 32:8 NKJV). Ask God to give you the power of His divine guidance, helping you fulfill His plan for your life. And remember that "the LORD [goes] before you" (Isaiah 52:12 NIV) into the days ahead, allowing you to "leave the Irreparable Past in His hands, and step out into the Irresistible Future with Him."[14]

I arise today, through. . .
God's eye to look before me.

My Desires

Delight thyself also in the LORD; and he shall
give thee the desires of thine heart.
PSALM 37:4 KJV

*L*ord, as I come before You today, delighting in Your presence, I ask for Your divine guidance. You know the desires of my heart—to know, love, and live in You. Show me the way You want me to go. Give me the courage to face the future, knowing that because You go before me, I need never be afraid.

Serving with Purpose

"David. . .served the purpose of God in his own generation."
ACTS 13:36 NASB

*D*earest God, You have a purpose for my life. You have plans to prosper me. I put my life, my heart, my spirit, and my soul in Your safe hands, this minute, this hour, this day. Within Your firm grasp, I need not worry about what tomorrow may bring. I know You have my life planned. I just need to keep close to You and to keep walking in Your way, looking neither to the right nor the left but straight ahead toward You.

Loved Now and Forever

I am convinced that neither death nor life, neither angels nor demons,
neither the present nor the future, nor any powers, neither height nor depth,
nor anything else in all creation, will be able to separate us from
the love of God that is in Christ Jesus our Lord.
ROMANS 8:38–39 NIV

*N*o matter what happens, Lord, I cannot be separated from You and Your love. Oh, what that means to me! Fill me with the love that never ends. May it flow through me and reach those I meet this day. May my future be filled with blessing upon blessing, and may I praise You today and in the days to come.

A Future for Me

Consider the blameless, observe the upright;
there is a future for the man of peace.
PSALM 37:37 NIV

*L*ord, I am Your child, a child of peace. When someone strikes me on the left cheek, I turn my head and give them the other. I can only do this through Your power. Nothing can harm me when I am living so close to You. Now, with the next breath I take, give me the gift of stillness, of silence, as I put my future, my hopes, my dreams into Your capable hands.

Sweet Wisdom Breeds Hope

So shall the knowledge of wisdom be unto thy soul: when thou hast found it, then there shall be a reward, and thy expectation shall not be cut off.

PROVERBS 24:14 KJV

*Y*ou, O Lord, give me hope for the future. Your presence fills me. I seek Your wisdom to renew my spirit and help me face the challenges of this life. I have great expectations. I believe that You are working in my life and good things await me today. May I further the plans for Your kingdom as You lead me through this life and time.

In God's Arms!

Then I said to you, "Do not be terrified; do not be afraid of them. The LORD your God, who is going before you, will fight for you, as he did for you in Egypt, before your very eyes, and in the desert. There you saw how the LORD your God carried you, as a father carries his son, all the way you went until you reached this place."

DEUTERONOMY 1:29–31 NIV

*N*o matter what I face today, You, Lord, are going before me. You appear before my very eyes. You will lead me through the desert, sustaining me with Your living water. When I am tired, You will carry me like a child, until I reach the place You have intended for me.

A Future Hope

There is surely a future hope for you, and your hope will not be cut off.
PROVERBS 23:18 NIV

*N*othing will cause me dismay, nothing will discourage me with You by my side, O Lord of my life. Help me to seek Your advice, Your Word, before I speak, before I move, before I act. Guide me through this maze of life, Lord, with the assurance that You always walk before me. Embed this truth deep within my soul.

No Fear for the Future

Keep sound wisdom and discretion: So shall they be life unto thy soul, and grace to thy neck. Then shalt thou walk in thy way safely, and thy foot shall not stumble. When thou liest down, thou shalt not be afraid: yea, thou shalt lie down, and thy sleep shall be sweet.
PROVERBS 3:21–24 KJV

*D*o not allow my foot to stumble, Lord. Eliminate the obstacles of worry and fear that line the path before me. Give me hope and courage to face my future. Give me a clear mind to make the right decisions. And, at the end of this day, give me the peace of sweet slumber as I lie down within Your mighty arms.

Unknown Future

Indeed, how can people avoid what they don't know is going to happen?
ECCLESIASTES 8:7 NLT

*D*ear God, I don't know what lies before me. I feel plagued by the what-ifs that tumble through my mind and pierce my confident spirit. Allow me to let You fill my soul. Help me to be confident in Your wisdom and power to guide me, so that, although You have concealed from me the knowledge of future events, I may be ready for any changes that may come.

Strengthened Hearts

"For the eyes of the LORD move to and fro throughout the earth that He may strongly support those whose heart is completely His."
2 CHRONICLES 16:9 NASB

*Y*our eyes, Lord, are ranging throughout the earth. You see it all, Lord, the past, the present, the future. You are the God that was, is, and will be. You are constantly looking out for me because my heart is fully committed to You. Help me to rest in the assurance that Your arms will always uphold me. I want to be with You forever and ever.

Trusting God

Trust in the LORD with all thine heart; and lean not unto thine own understanding. In all thy ways acknowledge him, and he shall direct thy paths.

PROVERBS 3:5–6 KJV

*L*ord, I don't understand what is happening in my life. I don't know what the future holds. I don't know where my path lies, what my next step should be. But I trust in You, Lord. In all my ways and days I acknowledge Your working in my life. I am confident that You will make my paths straight.

Shattered Plans

"My days have passed, my plans are shattered, and so are the desires of my heart."

JOB 17:11 NIV

O God, all my plans are in ruins. I don't understand why all this is happening. The things I have desired are out of my reach. I feel like Job. Yet at the end of his days, as he kept his confidence in You, You blessed Job, making his life even richer than before. Wipe the tears of frustration and disappointment from my eyes, Lord. Help me to keep my focus on You and not on my troubles or my worries about what the future will bring.

God's Plans

But the plans of the LORD stand firm forever,
the purposes of his heart through all generations.
PSALM 33:11 NIV

*Y*ou have led me to this place where I now lie before You, seeking Your presence and Your face, Your guidance and Your strength. Your plans for my life stand firm, although they are as yet unrevealed to me. With one glance, You see all the generations that have gone before, that are present now, and that will come in the future. You see it all! Allow me to rest in the knowledge that each and every day You go before me, and that in the end, all will be well with my soul.

Man's Plans, God's Purpose

Many plans are in a man's mind, but it is the Lord's purpose for him that will stand.
PROVERBS 19:21 AMP

*Y*ou know the plans of my mind and the desires of my heart, but as Your Word says, it is Your purpose that will rule the day. Help me to step aside if I am blocking Your way. Help me to keep confident in Your Word and in Your plan for my life. I await Your instructions for the day.

My Needs

The Power of Persistent, Specific, Expectant Petition

So I say to you, Ask and keep on asking and it shall be given you;
seek and keep on seeking and you shall find; knock and keep
on knocking and the door shall be opened to you.
LUKE 11:9 AMP

When we had to have our dog Schaefer put down, my family and I were heartbroken. That night and the next morning, I asked God to heal us from our grief and give us a new, healthy puppy to love. I continued this petition every morning in my quiet time with God.

The following week we brought home a six-month-old Springer spaniel mix from the local SPCA, which we named Ziggy. Within days, though, we realized our puppy was lame and very aggressive toward anyone other than our family. Weeks later our vet diagnosed Ziggy as having severe hip dysplasia. The vet's recommendation was either a hip replacement—a beyond-our-means surgical procedure with only a slim chance of successfully correcting his lameness—or having Ziggy put down. On the Monday after Thanksgiving, we chose the latter course.

Wounded but not defeated, we went looking for another puppy. Now my daily petitions were more desperate. Our family was reeling under the emotional trauma of having put down two dogs in less than a month. All we wanted was a healthy, affectionate puppy in need of a good home. Each day I continued to ask God to meet our need. At the same time, I didn't understand why we were led to buy the first puppy, only to have the situation end so tragically. But as I thought about it, I realized that perhaps we'd rushed into buying Ziggy because I was so desperate for a Springer spaniel, leading me to insist on the puppy I *wanted* instead of what our family *needed*.

So I decided to make my petition to God more specific. Now I told God that I didn't care what the puppy looked like, only that it be a healthy, loving, face-licking, eager-and-able-to-go-for-a-walk pound puppy. I also asked God for patience, to give me a waiting yet joyfully confident, expectant heart.

Just when we had about given up hope, my husband Pete urged my son Zach and me to check out the last puppy left at a local dog rescue facility. As we walked up the long driveway of Dogs for Adoption, a wrinkly-headed, yellow-haired puppy came loping along on the heels of one of the rescue workers. He had the head of a Shar-Pei and the body of a yellow Lab. As he ran to my son, he first licked his face and then nibbled on his ear, turning my sixteen-year-old teenager into a giggling, joyous boy. It was love at first sight.

That afternoon we brought home a healthy, loving, face-licking, eager-and-able-to-go-for-a-walk, yet amazingly funny-looking, mischievous puppy that gnaws on furniture, steals remote controls, chews up socks, shoes, and Christmas ornaments, and has more strength and energy than Superman. Praise God, our new dog Durham is more affectionate than we could have ever dreamed (he doesn't just sit *by* you, he sits *on* you). And with so much extra skin that you can continually reshape his face, head, and chin, he looks sillier than we could have imagined! In His timing and in His way, God answered my persistent, specific, expectant petitions.

Every day we are to ask the Lord to supply our needs (see Luke 11:3). Our petitions must be specific for "Jesus desires such definite prayer for our own sakes because it teaches us to know our own needs better."[15] And after we ask, we are to keep on asking, forever persevering in our prayers (like the bold friend in Luke 11:5–8 who needed bread for a guest, and the woman wanting judgment in Luke 18:1–5). And in the asking we are to be confident, trusting that He will indeed supply all we need (see Philippians 4:19). Then we are to wait expectantly for the Lord to fulfill those needs (see Micah 7:7) in His perfect timing—not ours (see Psalm 145:15).

Even in the midst of circumstances that appear to be tearing your heart apart, shredding your hope, and trampling your dreams, have faith. Look not behind but—with your hand in His—look forward. For what He will do in you is beyond all you can ask or imagine.

Harness the power of persistent, specific, expectant petitions. Present your needs to God today and every day— ask and keep on asking—remembering the words of Andrew Murray: "Let prayer be not only the utterance of your desires, but a fellowship with God, until we know by faith that our prayers are heard."[16]

I arise today, through. . .
God's ear to hear me.

Financial Aid

You do not have, because you do not ask God.
JAMES 4:2 NIV

*H*ere I am, Lord, coming to You to ask You to fill my needs, to help me to support my family financially. God, You know these are hard times, You know how much money this household needs to function each day, week, and month. Hear my prayer and help me to do my part in providing for my family. I thank You for this roof over our heads. And now I humbly beseech You to help us meet our needs.

Christ's Riches

My God shall supply all your need according to His riches in glory by Christ Jesus.
PHILIPPIANS 4:19 NKJV

*O*h, Lord, what a promise You have made to me, that You will supply all I need through Christ. He is my Good Shepherd; with Him I shall not want! Help me to rest confidently in the assurance that in Your time my prayers will be answered. Let my prayer time be more than utterances of what I desire but a time of fellowship with You, knowing that You will provide what I need.

51

Watching with Hope

*But as for me, I watch in hope for the LORD, I
wait for God my Savior; my God will hear me.*
MICAH 7:7 NIV

I watch and wait expectantly, Lord, for You to answer the
petitions I make to You today. I bring them to You mindful of
the way You are always there, ready to listen, ready to advise,
ready to answer. Give me the gift of patience as I wait for Your
response. Help me not to run ahead of You but to wait and
pray and hope.

Morning Requests

*In the morning You hear my voice, O Lord; in the morning I prepare [a prayer, a
sacrifice] for You and watch and wait [for You to speak to my heart].*
PSALM 5:3 AMP

*L*ord, here I am this morning, coming before You once again.
I know You hear my voice, but You even understand my groans
and know my unspoken thoughts. In this stillness, I present
my requests to You and I look to You for a reply. I watch for
Your presence to come near me. I wait for You to speak to my
heart, knowing that You only want what's best for me. Thank
You for being my loving, patient, and just heavenly Father.

In His Time

The LORD upholdeth all that fall, and raiseth up all those that be bowed down. The eyes of all wait upon thee; and thou givest them their meat in due season. Thou openest thine hand, and satisfiest the desire of every living thing.

PSALM 145:14–16 KJV

Lord, sometimes I don't understand why it takes so long for You to answer some of my prayers. At times Your answers are immediate, but on other occasions, I need to keep coming before You, asking over and over again for You to meet my need. Help me to grow during this time, Lord. Give me the confidence to ask and keep on asking.

Day by Day

Give us day by day our daily bread.

LUKE 11:3 KJV

You know what I need, Lord, and I am here before You again this morning, asking You to meet those needs. As food prices continue to rise, I need Your help more and more to feed my family. Help me to fill those mouths with which You have so graciously blessed me.

God's Goodness

"God has been very generous to me. I have more than enough."
GENESIS 33:11 NLT

*L*ord, I come to You this morning, thanking You for giving me all that I need each and every day. I have endured some lean times in the past, but right now, things are looking up, and it's all because I looked up—to You! Help me to keep my focus upon You and not on what I lack.

Lifting Manna

Each morning everyone gathered as much as he needed.
EXODUS 16:21 NIV

*H*ere I am once more, Lord, asking You again this morning to meet my needs. I've been so down, Lord, with all the things that have been happening in the world, in my home, in my family. Help me again today to go forth, to gather as much as I need and be content with that. Hear my prayer, O Lord, and help me day by day.

Boundless Grace

*God is able to make all grace (every favor and earthly blessing) come to you in
abundance, so that you may always and under all circumstances and whatever the
need be self-sufficient [possessing enough to require no aid or support and furnished in
abundance for every good work and charitable donation].*

2 CORINTHIANS 9:8 AMP

*L*ord, because of You, I have all I need. You continually shower
blessings upon me to the point where they are overflowing.
With Your support, I can finally stand on my own two feet.
I even have enough left over to give to others and to do the
work that You have called me to do. Thank You, Father, for
blessing my life.

Wounded Hearts

For I am poor and needy, and my heart is wounded within me.

PSALM 109:22 KJV

I hate being so needy, Lord, so poor, so hurt, so wounded.
Troubles plague me on each and every side every time I try
to depend upon myself to meet all my needs. Today I come to
You, the source of all power. Grant me my petitions. Help me
to rest assured that You are taking care of me, and that as long
as I abide in You, all will be well.

Night and Day

Now a true widow, a woman who is truly alone in this world, has placed her hope in God. She prays night and day, asking God for his help.

1 TIMOTHY 5:5 NLT

*L*ike the widow, Lord, I sometimes feel so alone, and so I put my trust in You. I come to You this morning, crying to You for help—financially, spiritually, emotionally, relationally, physically. I am in desperate need of You, my one and only source of hope! My hope today is on things unseen, remedies that You will bring to pass. As I rely on You, continue to feed my faith.

Sharing Abundance

" 'I needed clothes and you clothed me, I was sick and you looked after me, I was in prison and you came to visit me.' "

MATTHEW 25:36 NIV

*L*ord, as I present my needs to You, and as You meet those needs, remind me of the needs of others, realizing that I may be *Your* answer to someone else's prayer today.

Well-Watered Gardens

*And the L*ORD *shall guide thee continually, and satisfy thy soul in drought,*
and make fat thy bones: and thou shalt be like a watered garden,
and like a spring of water, whose waters fail not.
ISAIAH 58:11 KJV

*Y*ou are the source of my life. Day by day You have met my needs in this sun-scorched land afflicted with the heat of greed and intolerance. As I come to You with today's petitions, may I be reminded of the ways You have rescued me in the past, resting in the assurance that You will once again deliver me from my troubles. Right now, in Your presence, I feel Your life springing up within me. Thank You for Your living water that never fails.

Bold Petitioners

"I tell you, even though he will not get up and give him anything because he is his friend,
yet because of his persistence he will get up and give him as much as he needs."
LUKE 11:8 NASB

I boldly come to You this morning, knowing that You will give me as much as I need because of Your love for me. Thank You for guiding me, giving me wisdom, and teaching me patience. You have blessed me before, and I am confident that You will continue to bless me as I serve You.

My Praises

The Power of Adoration

Give thanks to him and praise his name.
PSALM 100:4 NLT

*W*hat a privilege to approach God, to bow down before Him, laud Him with our praises, and feel His presence within us! Sometimes, as we draw near, appropriate words evade us. Yet all is not lost for God has given us a powerful, praise-filled resource—the book of Psalms. Richard J. Foster writes, "The Psalms are the literature of worship and their most prominent feature is praise. 'Praise the Lord!' is the shout that reverberates from one end of the Psalter to the other. Singing, shouting, dancing, rejoicing, adoring—all are the language of praise."[17] Another author writes, "The Psalms magnify and praise the Lord, exalt His attributes, His name, His Word and His goodness."[18]

The act of raising our eyes and mouthing words of praise to God is essential to our spiritual life. Dear friends, God is *looking* for people to praise Him. Jesus said, "The true worshipers will worship the Father in spirit and truth; for such people the Father *seeks* to be His worshipers" (John 4:23 NASB, emphasis added).

In the midst of praising our Lord and Savior, our lives are transformed in several ways. First and foremost, our spirits become intimately connected with His. As we lift our voices, extolling His name and deeds, we are invaded by His presence. "But You are holy, O You Who dwell in [the holy place]...praises...[are offered]" (Psalm 22:3 AMP). God abides within us when we praise Him!

Second, when we praise God our fears are allayed. Psalm 56:10–11 says, "In God, whose word I praise, in the LORD, whose word I praise—in God I trust; I will not be afraid" (NIV). There is no room for fear where praise has taken up residence.

Third, praise changes our outlook as we view our world through the eyes of our Creator. "Praise the LORD from the heavens.... Let [His angels, heavenly hosts, sun, moon, stars, highest heavens, waters above the skies] praise the name of the LORD, for he commanded and they were created" (Psalm 148: 1, 5 NIV). Suddenly, when we see things from the perspective of the One who made and sustains the entire universe, the cares of this world grow dim.

Fourth, praise vanquishes our enemy. Second Chronicles 20 tells the story of when Jehoshaphat, king of Judah, was faced with a vast army coming against him. He prayed to the Lord, " 'We do not know what to do, but our eyes are upon you' " (verse 12 NIV). The people bowed down and worshiped the Lord. The next morning, Jehoshaphat appointed his men to sing to the Lord and praise His name. They went out into the front lines, ahead of the army, saying, " 'Give thanks to the LORD, for his love endures forever' " (verse 21 NIV). The result? Not only was that day's foe vanquished (the enemy armies ended up destroying each other), but for the remainder of Jehoshaphat's reign, "God [gave] him rest on every side" (verse 30 NIV).

And finally, our love for God is deepened when we adore Him and give Him thanks for past blessings. It is then we are reminded that "for as high as the heavens are above the earth, so great is the measure of our Father's love."[19]

After the sun rises but before you approach God with

your daily petitions, get into the praise mode, reminding Him (and yourself) how terrific He really is, how awed you are to have Him in your life, how blessed you are that He came down to earth to save *you*. Drench yourself in the words of praise amid the Psalms. Sing a familiar worship song at the top of your lungs! Have no reservations as you come into His presence, glorifying His name. And as you speak to your Creator, through His Word, He will speak to you.

I arise today, through. . .
God's word to speak to me.

Shouting for Joy!

Be glad in the LORD and rejoice, you righteous;
and shout for joy, all you upright in heart!
PSALM 32:11 NKJV

*Y*our hands created the heavens and the earth. You breathed upon Adam and gave him life. Everything that was created was created through Your Son Jesus Christ. The trees, the earth, the waters, and the creatures clap their hands in praise to You. This is the day that You have made! I will rejoice and be glad in it as I shout Your name to the heavens!

Praising in Song

My heart greatly rejoiceth; and with my song will I praise him.
PSALM 28:7 KJV

*M*y heart rejoices in Your presence this morning! To Your ears, Lord, I pray that my singing will be a joyful noise. Your grace is amazing. You are my all in all, I worship and adore You. Lean down Your ear to me as I sing about Your love, for how great Thou art, Lord! How great Thou art!

An Answer to My Cry

Come and listen, all you who fear God; let me tell you what he has done for me. I cried out to him with my mouth; his praise was on my tongue. . . . God has surely listened and heard my voice in prayer. Praise be to God!

PSALM 66:16–17, 19–20 NIV

*D*ear God, You have done so many things for me, saved me from so many dangers, toils, and snares. I cry out to You again this morning. Fill me with Your Spirit. Touch me with Your presence. And as I go through this day, may I be so filled with Your praises that I cannot help but tell others what You have done for me!

By His Great Mercy

In the morning, O LORD, you hear my voice. . . . I, by your great mercy. . .come into your house; in reverence. . .I bow down toward your holy temple.

PSALM 5:3, 7 NIV

*L*ord, I humble myself before You, bowing down at Your throne. You are so great, so awesome. Your presence fills this universe. I am filled with Your amazing love, touched by Your compassion. There is no one like You in my life, my Master, my Lord, my God.

Praise Silences Enemies

From the lips of children and infants you have ordained praise because of your enemies,
to silence the foe and the avenger.

PSALM 8:2 NIV

With You on my side, You who hold the heavens in Your hands, You who sustain the entire universe, I need not be afraid of my enemies, of those who wish to harm me, or of the evil one that dogs my steps. With praises to You on my lips and in my heart, my foes are vanquished. You are my great refuge, my rock of strength.

His Awesome Power

Say to God, "How awesome are your deeds! So great is your power.... All the earth
bows down to you; they sing praise to you, they sing praise to your name."

PSALM 66:3–4 NIV

Lord, You parted the Red Sea and You still the wind and the waves. You give sight to the blind and hearing to the deaf. You raise people from the dead. Your power is awesome. Nothing is impossible for You. I bow before You, singing praises to Your name.

Praise for Deliverance

I will praise you, O Lord my God, with all my heart; I will glorify your name forever.
For great is your love toward me; you have delivered me from the depths of the grave.
PSALM 86:12–13 NIV

*Y*ou are the Good Shepherd, the All-Sufficient One, my Rock of Refuge. You hold the universe in Your hands and yet You are concerned with everything going on in my life. I am staggered by Your love and faithfulness to me. You continually draw me up into Your presence. You deliver me from the depths of darkness.

No Fear When God Is Near

In God will I praise his word: in the LORD will I praise his word. In God have I put my trust: I will not be afraid what man can do unto me.
PSALM 56:10–11 KJV

*Y*our instruction keeps me on the right path and for that I praise You. Thank You for giving me Your Holy Word, to have and to hold. With Your Word I can speak to You and You can speak to me. You are the Great Communicator of my life. I trust in Your Word, for when I am armed with it, I have no fear.

Heart-Filled Praise

I will praise thee with my whole heart. . . . I will worship toward thy holy temple, and
praise thy name for thy lovingkindness and for thy truth:
for thou hast magnified thy word above all thy name.

PSALM 138:1–2 KJV

As I sit here before You, my heart reaches out to touch You, the great God, seated in the heavenlies. Meld my spirit with Yours so that our wills are one. Your love and faithfulness are tremendous. I praise You, Lord, with my lips, my voice, my mouth, my life.

Lifelong Praise

I will sing unto the LORD as long as I live: I will sing
praise to my God while I have my being.

PSALM 104:33 KJV

At this moment and throughout this day, I sing my praises to You, O God. Music is one of Your gifts and I thank You for it. As my spirit in song rises to join with Yours, may I continually be reminded of all You are, of all You have done, and all You will do.

Praise to the Heavenly Creator

Bless the LORD, O my soul! O LORD my God, You are very great: You are clothed with honor and majesty, who cover Yourself with light as with a garment, who stretch out the heavens like a curtain. He lays the beams of His upper chambers in the waters, who makes the clouds His chariot, who walks on the wings of the wind.

PSALM 104:1–3 NKJV

*Y*ou made all the planets, all the stars, the waters on the earth, the land on which I stand. Is there nothing too difficult for You? You are wrapped in light, and I come now into that light, to be with You, to revel in Your presence, to praise Your holy name. Surround me with Your arms among these clouds.

Praise for Forgiveness and Healing

Let all that I am praise the LORD; may I never forget the good things he does for me. He forgives all my sins and heals all my diseases.

PSALM 103:2–3 NLT

*D*ear Lord, You have given Your one and only Son to die for me. Because of You and Your great gift, I have eternal life. You have forgiven my sins and healed my soul. Nothing is impossible with You in my life. Thank You for taking care of me. With all that I am, with my entire being, I praise You forever and ever!

Praise for Strength

O my strength, I will sing praises to You; for God is my stronghold,
the God who shows me lovingkindness.

PSALM 59:17 NASB

When I am weak, Your strength upholds me. When I am afraid, Your courage sustains me. When I am downcast, Your presence uplifts me. You are always there for me. How great, how wonderful, how amazing You are, my God, my Friend, my Father. I am here before You, singing endless praises to Your name!

Praise for His Gifts!

Sing to God, sing praises to His name, cast up a highway for Him Who rides through
the deserts — His name is the Lord — be in high spirits and glory before Him!

PSALM 68:4 AMP

I am in high spirits today, Lord. You have provided all that I need and more! Along with my earthly needs, You have provided me with grace, spiritual gifts, love, forgiveness, Your Word, Your Son. My heart is so light. I come to You singing praises and I leave with a smile on my lips. In Your presence, my spirit is lifted. Praise the Lord!

My World

The Power of Compassion

Therefore, as God's chosen people, holy and dearly loved, clothe yourselves with compassion, kindness, humility, gentleness and patience.

COLOSSIANS 3:12 NIV

Compassion is defined by *Merriam-Webster's Dictionary* as "sympathetic consciousness of others' distress together with a desire to alleviate it." Our God is the Father of compassion. He had so much sympathy for our suffering that He sent His one and only Son to die for us (see John 3:16). Do you share God's compassion? Do you realize that "Jesus Christ wants to express through you what the Father expressed through Him, bringing love and hope to a hurting world"[20]? We, God's people, are to be clothed with compassion (see Colossians 3:12). What are you wearing today?

Some of us, when our tender hearts see the troubles of others, may think we are too far away or too powerless to help. But that is an untruth. Our prayers are full of heavenly power. They transcend time and space. We can be on our knees in our living rooms and reach a president in the White House, a homeless man on a city street, children starving in North Korea, missionaries in South America, or an AIDS worker in Africa. With the power of compassion combined with prayer, *we can make a difference*!

John Hull writes, "Praying to make a difference is unselfish praying...[and] in all likelihood is going to cost us something. It's probably going to make us uncomfortable and take us to places—spiritually and geographically—where we wouldn't dare go unless God had birthed it in our hearts. . . . Praying to make a difference in this world means we learn to get past ourselves and our problems and pursue a greater purpose."[21]

Nehemiah was an unselfish man of prayer who looked beyond himself and his needs. His example shows us what we need to do to be powerful intercessors for this world. Like Nehemiah, we need to find out what is happening outside the sphere of me, myself, and I. When Nehemiah met Hanani, one of his brothers who had come from Judah, Nehemiah *asked for news* of the Jews in Jerusalem. It was then that he found out the specifics of the remnant's desperate situation, how the wall of Jerusalem was broken down, leaving the Jews defenseless against their enemies (see Nehemiah 1:1–3).

As soon as he heard of their situation, Nehemiah sat down and wept. *He felt compassion* and his heart mourned. The Bible says he fasted and *prayed*, asking God to hear him, remember His promises to His people, and give him success (see Nehemiah 1:4–11).

A few months later Nehemiah took wine to King Artaxerxes, and with one look at his cupbearer's face, which revealed "sadness of heart," the king inquired as to Nehemiah's troubles, asking what he could do for him. Here Nehemiah *took direct action* as he reached out to another. Through that assistance, he was able to personally assess the situation in Jerusalem and, ultimately, to help rebuild the wall.

Nehemiah was *filled with faith*, telling those who later ridiculed the rebuilding, " 'The God of heaven will give us success' " (Nehemiah 2:20 NIV).

What walls can you help rebuild? What needs do you see outside of yourself? For what areas—your church, your school, your government—is God prompting you to pray? To what dire situations—world hunger, terrorism, war, crime—is your heart drawn?

When you hear of distress in the world and your heart responds with compassion, make a difference! Get down on your knees and pray with persistence. And if so led, take direct action. Be filled with confidence that God will work in the situation.

In this world, Jesus says we will have trouble. When things seem hopeless, we must be confident that Christ will meet us in the fire, as He did Shadrach, Meshach, and Abednego. When terror seems to reign on every side, continue faithfully onward, remembering that "if we are thrown into the blazing furnace, the God we serve is able to save us from it, and he will rescue us" (Daniel 3:17 NIV). Because of His unfailing compassion, we will not be consumed (see Lamentations 3:22).

I arise today, through. . .
God's hand to guard me.

Praise for the Father of Compassion

Blessed be the God and Father of our Lord Jesus Christ,
the Father of mercies and God of all comfort.
2 CORINTHIANS 1:3 NKJV

*L*ord, You love us so much. Fill me with that love to overflowing. Give me a compassionate heart. Lead me to the concern You would like me to champion for You, whether it be working in a soup kitchen, helping the homeless, or adopting a missionary couple. Lead me in prayer as I go down on my knees and intercede for others in distress.

Intercession for World Leaders

First of all, then, I urge that entreaties and prayers, petitions and thanksgivings, be
made on behalf of all men, for kings and all who are in authority, so that we may lead a
tranquil and quiet life in all godliness and dignity.
1 TIMOTHY 2:1–2 NASB

*D*ear God, today I lift up the world leaders—presidents, premiers, kings, queens, prime ministers, ambassadors to the United Nations, all rulers, princes, and governors. Give them wisdom, give them courage, give them minds of peace. There is so much death and destruction in this world and at times I feel disheartened. But I know where to turn—to You, my Father, who makes all things right.

Perseverance in Prayer

*As you know, we consider blessed those who have persevered. You have heard of Job's
perseverance and have seen what the Lord finally brought about.
The Lord is full of compassion and mercy.*

JAMES 5:11 NIV

I feel like I've been praying forever for a situation that does
not seem to be changing, Lord. I feel like Job: Here I am on
my knees in prayer while the entire world dissolves around
me. But I know that You are in control. You know all things.
So once again, I lift my concern up to You, confident that You
will handle the situation in Your timing.

God's Hand Guarding Us

*I pray not that thou shouldest take them out of the world, but that thou shouldest keep
them from the evil. They are not of the world, even as I am not of the world. As thou
hast sent me into the world, even so have I also sent them into the world.*

JOHN 17:15–16, 18 KJV

*L*ord, sometimes I feel like Captain Kirk. When faced with
the evils of this world, I want to say, "Beam me up, God!"
But I know that no matter what happens in this world, Your
hand is guarding us. And armed with Your compassion, we
have the power to intercede for the hungry, the oppressed, the
imprisoned, the homeless, the wounded.

Reigning Peace

[Jesus said,] These things I have spoken unto you, that in me ye might have peace. In the world ye shall have tribulation: but be of good cheer; I have overcome the world.

JOHN 16:33 KJV

*D*ear God, how I pray for peace around the world. Some say it's impossible—but with You all things are possible. And while peace may not yet reign throughout the earth, with You in my heart, peace reigns within, for You have overcome the world! May all people feel Your peace within!

Compassion for the Hungry

Is there any encouragement from belonging to Christ? Any comfort from his love? Any fellowship together in the Spirit? Are your hearts tender and compassionate? Then make me truly happy by agreeing wholeheartedly with each other, loving one another, and working together with one mind and purpose.

PHILIPPIANS 2:1–2 NLT

*W*ith the compassion You show to us, Your abiding tenderness through thick and thin, today I reach out to the hungry here and abroad. Open up my eyes to how I can help. Show me where my hands can be used to help feed those who are starving. I want to serve others in the name of Jesus Christ, for that is what You have called us to do. Open a door for me. Show me what I can do to make this world a better place.

Praise for Forgiveness and Healing

The weapons we fight with are not the weapons of the world. On the contrary,
they have divine power to demolish strongholds.

2 CORINTHIANS 10:4 NIV

*G*od, through the divine power of Your Spirit and Your Word, I pray for my neighborhood. Demolish the stronghold of evil within this community. Touch each heart with Your peace and understanding. You know what each family needs. Help me to be an encouragement to them. Be with me as I take a prayer walk around this neighborhood, lifting each family up to Your heavenly throne.

Comfort for the Suffering

[Jesus said,] "You are the light of the world —
like a city on a hilltop that cannot be hidden."

MATTHEW 5:14 NLT

*D*earest Christ, I pray for Your bright, shining light to spread out into the world. For Your love to reach the ends of the earth. Give comfort to those who suffer from abuse and violence. Touch them with Your healing light and guard them with Your protective hand. Give them assurance that You are there. Allow them to feel Your presence, hear Your voice, feel Your touch.

Change the Hearts of Terrorists

Finally, all of you, live in harmony with one another; be sympathetic,
love as brothers, be compassionate and humble.

1 PETER 3:8 NIV

*D*ear Lord, please soften the calloused hearts of those who deem themselves terrorists. Exchange their hearts of stone for ones tender with love. Protect the innocent here and abroad, especially missionaries who risk their lives to spread Your light. Comfort those who have lost loved ones through the violence around the world. Lord, can't we all just get along?

Victory for Youth

For our struggle is not against flesh and blood, but against the rulers, against the
powers, against the world forces of this darkness, against
the spiritual forces of wickedness in the heavenly places.

EPHESIANS 6:12 NASB

*L*ord, I pray that You would oust the unseen evils from this land, that Your angels would battle fiercely against the dark forces corrupting our youth. Empower our youth leaders to claim a victory for young hearts. Show me how I can help at my church, how I can lead teens to You. Give parents the right words to say when dealing with their children.

Protection for Missionaries and Pastors

"If it be so, our God whom we serve is able to deliver us
from the furnace of blazing fire; and He will deliver us."
DANIEL 3:17 NASB

I pray for others with the confidence that You, dear Lord, hear my prayer. That although at times this world seems so unsettled, Your hand is upon our missionaries and pastors, guarding them when they are awake and as they sleep. Give them the strength to do what You have called them to do. Give them the means to help the lost, starving, diseased, and imprisoned. Give them wisdom as they reveal Your Word and reach into the darkness to spread Your light.

Message of Eternal Life

The world and its desires pass away, but the
man who does the will of God lives forever.
1 JOHN 2:17 NIV

*T*he world may pass away, but Your love never fails. Those who believe in You will live with You forever. What a blessed thing! I pray that others around the world will hear the message so that they, too, can accept Your gift of eternal life. Show me how I can help spread the message, all to Your glory.

Clothed with Compassion

Therefore, as God's chosen people, holy and dearly loved, clothe yourselves with compassion, kindness, humility, gentleness and patience.
COLOSSIANS 3:12 NIV

As I get down on my knees, I wrap myself within the cloak of compassion. I bring to You specific concerns for which You have led me to pray, knowing that You hear my prayer, confident that You will answer. And as I rise from the place of prayer, may Your kindness, humility, gentleness, and patience shine through me and lighten the hearts of others. I want to be Your servant. Help me to change the world.

Home, School, and Streets

You are of God, little children, and have overcome them, because He who is in you is greater than he who is in the world.
1 JOHN 4:4 NKJV

Lord, there are so many dark forces within our schools, on the streets, and even in our homes. I pray for Your light to eliminate the evil among us. I know that no matter what, You will prevail, dear Jesus. You have overcome this world. You have the power to do the impossible. Show me how I can make this world a better place. Give me the heart to intercede for others and the courage to step in when and where I am needed.

The Power of Active Faith

Faith by itself, if it is not accompanied by action, is dead.
JAMES 2:17 NIV

*W*hen I was a child, I saw only one minister in my church. He stood in the front of the sanctuary where he read and preached the Word of God while the rest of us sat facing him in the pews. But in the church I belong to today, I see many ministers every Sunday—ushers, singers, musicians, Sunday school teachers, sound room technicians, youth pastors, people of prayer, club leaders, kitchen workers, board members, teachers' aides, evangelism team members, and greeters. Everyone has their own spiritual gift they can use to serve or minister to others.

E. M. Bounds writes, "In carrying on his great work in the world, God works through human agents. He works through his church collectively and through his people individually. In order that they might be effective agents, they must be 'vessels unto honor, sanctified, and meet for the master's use, and prepared unto every good work.' "[22]

Sound scary? Feeling as if you're not "holy" enough to serve others? Relax. You are *already* holy and sanctified because you have faith in Jesus Christ and have accepted Him as your Savior (see 1 Corinthians 1:2; Ephesians 1:4). Through Christ, God created you and set you apart to do good works (see Ephesians 2:10). Andrew Murray writes, "Every believer is a laborer. As God's children, we have been redeemed for service and have our work waiting."[23]

So it appears there is no excuse for *not* serving God.

Perhaps the problem is that we are not sure what God has called us to do. Not even Paul was certain as to his role in God's plan. "What shall I do, Lord?" he asked. And God answered, "Get up. . .and go into Damascus. There you will be told all that you have been assigned to do." (See Acts 22:10.)

God has an assignment for each and every one of us. All we have to do is ask Him where and how He would like us to serve. Our gifts need not be limited to those listed in 1 Corinthians 12:8–10. The Church also needs those gifted in writing, music, hospitality, teaching, preaching, intercessory prayer, and missions, to name a few.

God doesn't want you just sitting in the pew every Sunday as you watch others ministering to your needs. According to His plan, although you are important to Him, it's not all about *you*. It's all about *God*. In *The Purpose-Driven Life*, Rick Warren writes, "You weren't created just to consume resources—to eat, breathe, and take up space. God designed you to make a difference with your life. . . . You were created to *add* to life on earth, not just take from it. God wants you to give something back. This is God's. . .purpose for your life, and it is called your 'ministry' or service."[24]

Find your spiritual gifts, ones that you love to use, so that you will be filled with a passion to serve. And then use them to God's great glory.

I arise today, through. . .
God's way to lie before me.

Living Sacrifices

Therefore, I urge you, brothers, in view of God's mercy, to offer your bodies as living sacrifices, holy and pleasing to God—this is your spiritual act of worship.
ROMANS 12:1 NIV

*H*ere I am, Lord, lifting myself up to You this morning. I want to serve You. I live to please You, for I love You with all my strength, soul, mind, heart, and body. I dedicate myself, my time, and my service to You. Show me the path You want me to take so that at the end of my days, when I see Your smiling face, You will say, "She did what she could."

Finding Your Gift

Don't act thoughtlessly, but understand what the Lord wants you to do.
EPHESIANS 5:17 NLT

*L*ord, I'm looking for direction. I'm not sure how You want me to serve You. So many times I feel so inadequate, that others can do things better than I ever could. But I know those feelings are not of You. Help me to understand, Lord, how You want me to serve, what You want me to do. Not worrying about pleasing others but pleasing You, I will do so all to Your glory.

Serving from the Heart

As slaves of Christ, do the will of God with all your heart.
EPHESIANS 6:6 NLT

I want to work for You, Lord, using all my heart, soul, and talent. I want to be Your tool, serving You with passion. And as I do so, help me to keep my eye and focus on You, and not on the gift You have given me. Help me to understand what You have shaped me to do.

Created for Good Works

We are God's masterpiece. He has created us anew in Christ Jesus, so we can do the good things he planned for us long ago.
EPHESIANS 2:10 NLT

*Y*ou have shaped me into the unique person I am today. You have created me to do good works. I am awed that You prepared things in advance for me to do. From the very beginning, You made me for a specific job in Your kingdom. Give me the courage to take hold of that task. Help me not to shy away from the challenges that face me.

Community Peace and Understanding

There are different kinds of gifts, but the same Spirit. There are different kinds of service, but the same Lord. There are different kinds of working, but the same God works all of them in all men.

1 CORINTHIANS 12:4–6 NIV

*G*ive me the humility You had when You washed the feet of the disciples. I am willing to take on whatever task—high or low—that You have for me. Grant me the spirit of cooperation as I work with others. Show me to how to use my gift in new and different ways. I serve to bring glory and honor and blessing to You.

On Assignment from God

The Lord has assigned to each his task.

1 CORINTHIANS 3:5 NIV

I come to You this morning asking for today's assignment. How would You have me serve You? Should I join the worship team? Should I become a prayer partner? Should I help in children's church? Show me the way that lies before me, Lord, so I can best serve You and others.

Serving the Lord

Whatever you do, do your work heartily, as for the Lord rather than for men,
knowing that from the Lord you will receive the reward of the inheritance.
It is the Lord Christ whom you serve.
COLOSSIANS 3:23–24 NASB

*S*ome days, Lord, I feel as if I am working to please others and not You. But that's not what it is all about. It is You I am serving, only You. You give me the power to do Your will. It is from You that I receive my reward for a job well done. Thank You, God, for giving me the opportunity to serve You and You alone!

Equipped for Service

May [God] equip you with all you need for doing his will. May he produce in you,
through the power of Jesus Christ, every good thing that is pleasing to him.
All glory to him forever and ever! Amen.
HEBREWS 13:21 NLT

*Y*ou have given me all that I need to do Your will. How great is that! Through the power of Jesus Christ, I can do anything You want me to do. Today I feel strong, bold, fearless. I am ready, willing, and able to do all that You call me to do this moment, this hour, this day.

Servants on Fire

Fan into flame the gift of God, which is in you.
2 TIMOTHY 1:6 NIV

Give me the passion, Lord, to serve You with the gifts You have given me. Reignite the enthusiasm I felt when I first began to serve You. Help me to forget about myself and to see only You. Help me to feel Your presence within me. Set me on fire for You and You alone!

Working As One

In Christ we who are many form one body, and each member belongs to all the others. We have different gifts, according to the grace given us.
ROMANS 12:5–6 NIV

Together we serve You, each one of us bringing our own unique gifts to lay at Your feet. Help me to do my best for You, to bring You glory, to spread Your light and Your love all around me and upon everything I touch.

Honoring God

God bought you with a high price. So you must honor God with your body.
1 CORINTHIANS 6:20 NLT

*R*emind me, Lord, that my service to You is a way to honor You with my body. You have done so much for me that it is overwhelming at times. Allow me to use my gift to bring greater glory to Your name so that others will be drawn ever closer to You.

Helping Each Other

A spiritual gift is given to each of us so we can help each other.
1 CORINTHIANS 12:7 NLT

*L*ord, my gift not only serves You but helps others as well. What a blessing! Be with me as I sacrifice my time and energy today to minister to others. This is my calling. This is my gift. And I do it all in Your love.

Here to Serve

*"For even the Son of Man came not to be served but to
serve others and to give his life as a ransom for many."*
MATTHEW 20:28 NLT

*W*hen You washed the feet of the disciples, that was a lesson for all of us. Your act of humble service brings tears to my eyes and a rush of warmth to my heart. May my service in Your name be as pleasing to You, as warming to Your heart and the hearts of those I touch.

Joyful Service

Serve the LORD with gladness.
PSALM 100:2 NKJV

*W*hat an awesome privilege to serve others! I welcome this opportunity. I go into my ministry with a smile on my face and a psalm in my heart. Thank You, God, for allowing me to do for others what You have done for me. I am so blessed!

The Power of Christ and His Sufficient Grace

[Christ] said to me, "My grace is sufficient for you,
for My strength is made perfect in weakness."
Therefore most gladly I will rather boast in my infirmities,
that the power of Christ may rest upon me. . . .
For when I am weak, then I am strong.
2 CORINTHIANS 12:9–10 NKJV

Whether we're feeling under the weather or something a bit more serious is afoot, we need to act in accordance with James 5:13–16. First go to the Lord in prayer. Then ask members of the church for prayer and anointing. And after that. . .well, what do we do when healing does not take place?

I first met my friend and mentor Glenn Garis eleven years ago. It was on a cold December night when I took my then five-year-old son Zach to the Silverdale Church to see the donkey, lambs, and calf in a live nativity scene. As we stood outside, shivering in the cold, people invited us to come into the church basement for cocoa and cookies. There was no saying "no" once Zach heard the word *cookies*. Once down the steps and through the double doors, Zach and I were approached by a well-dressed, older man with glasses and a receding hairline. Smiling, he extended his hand, saying, "Hi, my name is Glenn. Welcome to the Silverdale Church. God loves you."

My first thought was, *How does this guy know God loves me? What nerve.* My next thought was to leave the church basement as soon as possible. But Glenn had planted a seed.

The result? I attended my first worship service at Silverdale months later and have been going there ever since. During that time I got to know Glenn. He was a leader in the community and church, a positive thinker, a man of prayer, and a soul in love with God.

Years later Glenn was stricken with cancer. Through many prayers and anointings, a change of diet, medical treatments, and so on, Glenn won the first battle. But when the cancer later reappeared, he succumbed to the illness—but won the admiration of all those around him. During Glenn's illness, Christ gave him His grace, empowering him to change the lives of others—including his doctors—because of his obvious, unwavering faith. It was evident that the closer Glenn got to death, the more power he gained because the weaker he grew physically, the stronger he became spiritually. Like the man who was born blind and then healed by Jesus, "this happened so that the work of God might be displayed" (see John 9:1–3).

When we trust God, pray in His name, allow Him to transform us, rest in His loving arms, turn to Him for strength, and cling to the truth of His Word, we can find power and blessing even in the midst of our infirmities. In his book *How Can I Ask God for Physical Healing?* David J. Smith writes, "Acknowledge that God is sovereign. Commit yourself to the Lord. Wait patiently for Him to act. Seek professional medical attention if necessary. Realize that it may not be God's will for you to be healed. Ask the Lord for faith, patience, and wisdom. Pray that your circumstances will work out for the glory of God. [Then] *abandon yourself to divine providence.*"[25]

In sickness and in health, fortify your faith and strengthen your spirit by spending time in prayer, reading God's Word, and memorizing scripture. When feeling well, take care of your physical body by eating right, having regular check-ups, and getting plenty of exercise. As Charles H. Spurgeon said, "A mouthful of sea air, or a stiff walk in the wind's face, would not give grace to the soul, but it would yield oxygen to the body, which is the next best thing."[26]

Each day allow Christ to enter into your life, to transform you. Don't wait until you are gravely ill, with nowhere else to turn, to really understand and know the power of Christ and His grace. C. S. Lewis writes, "Everyone has noticed how hard it is to turn our thought to God when everything is going well with us. . . . We find God an interruption. . . . Or as a friend of mine said, 'We regard God as an airman regards his parachute; it's there for emergencies but he hopes he'll never have to use it.' "[27]

Through daily prayer, soak yourself in God's power and grace moment by moment. Spend time praising and thanking the Lord who heals you (see Exodus 15:26; James 5:13). Be like Daniel who "needed a miracle but never panicked. He just kept communing with God as he always had. He trusted that God was in control, no matter how bad the situation appeared. . . . Lost in the wonder of God [Daniel] kept praying"[28] (see Daniel 6:10).

Pray for the power of Christ's grace to rest upon you, for God's shield to protect the mind, body, and spirit of you and those He brings to your mind. And throughout your days, "Dear friend, I pray that you may enjoy good health and that all may go well with you, even as your soul is getting along well" (3 John 1:2 NIV).

I arise today, through. . .
God's shield to protect me.

One-Touch Healing

For she said within herself, If I may but touch his garment, I shall be whole.
MATTHEW 9:21 KJV

*D*ear God, I am reaching out my hand to You this morning, knowing that if I can just touch the hem of Your garment, You will make me whole. I envision You before me. I see the compassion in Your eyes. I know that You love me and that nothing is impossible for You. Fill me with Your love. Give me Your healing touch this morning.

Prayers Offered in Faith

Is anyone among you sick? Then he must call for the elders of the church and they are to pray over him, anointing him with oil in the name of the Lord; and the prayer offered in faith will restore the one who is sick.
JAMES 5:14–15 NASB

*L*ord, I am feeling so poorly. You know what is attacking my body. You can see everything. I ask you in prayer, right now, to fill me with Your healing light. Banish the sickness from my body. Fill me with Your presence. Draw me unto You.

The Healing Edge

People. . .begged him to let the sick just touch the edge of his cloak,
and all who touched him were healed.
MATTHEW 14:35-36 NIV

*L*ord, when I connect with You, when my body is filled with Your power and love, nothing can harm me. I am healed from within. Fill me now with Your presence. Heal my body, soul, and spirit. I praise Your name, for You are the one that heals me, saves me, loves me! Thank You for giving me life!

Strength in Weakness

Therefore I take pleasure in infirmities, in reproaches, in needs, in persecutions, in
distresses, for Christ's sake. For when I am weak, then I am strong.
2 CORINTHIANS 12:10 NKJV

*I*t's a paradox, but it is Your truth. When I am weak, I am strong because Your strength is made perfect in my weakness. Because You are in my life, I can rest in You. With Your loving arms around me, I am buoyed in spirit, soul, and body. When I am with You there is peace and comfort.

Crying Out for Healing

So Moses cried out to the LORD, "O God, please heal her!"
NUMBERS 12:13 NIV

*L*ord, when Miriam had leprosy, her brother cried out for her healing. I come to You this morning, crying out for You to heal my loved one. She is in so much pain. She needs your comfort, strength, love, and grace. Dear Lord, touch her! Allow her to feel Your presence. Immerse her in Your healing light.

His Promise of Restoration and Health

For I will restore health to you, and I will heal your wounds, says the Lord.
JEREMIAH 30:17 AMP

*Y*ou are the healer of our wounds, the One who restores spirit, soul, and body. Thank You for blessing my life. As I spend this time with You, I feel Your touch upon me. You are my gentle Shepherd, always trying to keep me from harm. Thank You, Jesus, for coming into my life, for making me complete, for restoring me to God. All praise and glory to my *Jehova-rapha*, the Lord who heals!

Relentless Praying

[Daniel] continued kneeling on his knees three times a day, praying and giving thanks before his God, as he had been doing previously.
DANIEL 6:10 NASB

"*A*s he had been doing previously"—what amazing words! Help me to be like Daniel, Lord. When faced with arrest and execution, when all seemed bleak and hopeless, he didn't panic but did as he had always done. He came before You on his knees, giving thanks. Keep me close to You, Lord. Enter my heart as I kneel at Your throne.

Healer of Hearts, Binder of Wounds

He heals the brokenhearted and binds up their wounds.
PSALM 147:3 NASB

*M*y heart is broken. I no longer have any strength. Fill me with Your power. Put Your arms around me. Let me linger in Your presence, bask in Your love. You are all I need. For without You, I can do nothing. Quench my thirst with Your living water. Feed me with Your bread of life. Nourish me deep within. I come to You in despair. I leave filled with joy.

Looking for His Heart

"For the eyes of the LORD move to and fro throughout the earth that He may strongly support those whose heart is completely His."

2 CHRONICLES 16:9 NASB

*H*ere I am, Lord! As you look for those whose hearts are completely Yours, here I am. Look at me, be with me. Support me in this time of need. You know my situation. You know what needs Your healing touch. As I rest silently before You, help me to be still and know You are God. You are my hope, my life, my peace.

Praise Ye the Lord!

Heal me, O LORD, and I will be healed; save me and I will be saved, for you are the one I praise.

JEREMIAH 17:14 NIV

I know that You are the source of all healing. Hold me in the palm of Your hand. Fill my mind, body, and soul with Your presence. I praise You, Lord, for all You have done, are doing, and will do for me! And I praise You for what you are. . .a loving God who is watching over me. Thank You, God. You are so good to me.

With All That Is within Me

Bless the LORD, O my soul; and all that is within me, bless His holy name!
Bless the LORD, O my soul, and forget not all His benefits:
who forgives all your iniquities, who heals all your diseases.
PSALM 103:1–3 NKJV

*E*verything I am, all that is within me, I draw upon as I praise Your holy name. You have done so many great things and have given me the power to do even greater things as I allow You to live through me. Thank You for healing me, for forgiving me. You are an awesome God!

You Have Heard My Prayers

" 'This is what the LORD, the God of your father David, says:
I have heard your prayer and seen your tears; I will heal you.' "
2 KINGS 20:5 NIV

*A*s I come to You today, I know that You hear the prayers and praises I offer. You have seen my tears. You know the calamity that has befallen me. You are my all in all. Give me the strength to endure this pain. Give me Your healing touch. Fill me with Your light and life. I thank You for working in my life, moment by moment, day by day.

With God, Everything Is Possible

Jesus looked at them and said, "With man this is impossible,
but with God all things are possible."
MATTHEW 19:26 NIV

*L*ord, knowing that You are in my life, I know I will be all right. Nothing can harm me with You by my side. You can do anything, Lord. Let Your glory shine through me so that others can see You within my earthly shell. Praise to the God who heals me and has made me whole!

I Want to Be Like Jesus

And we know that in all things God works for the good of those who love him,
who have been called according to his purpose. For those God foreknew he also
predestined to be conformed to the likeness of his Son.
ROMANS 8:28–29 NIV

*L*ord, I know that You will work everything out according to Your glory, according to Your will. I feel privileged that You have chosen me to serve You, that You have called me to this life. I want to be like You. Give me the strength of Christ, for His grace is sufficient for me. Thank You for hearing my prayer. O my soul, rejoice!

The Power of Confidence in Christ

And they who know Your name [who have experience and acquaintance with Your mercy] will lean on and confidently put their trust in You, for You, Lord, have not forsaken those who seek (inquire of and for) You.

PSALM 9:10 AMP

*F*ear comes in many sizes, shapes, and forms. There's a writer's fear of facing a blank page, a mother's fear of harm coming to her child, a father's fear of losing his job, a grandfather's fear of death, a banker's fear of being robbed, a soldier's fear of being killed, a country's fear of terrorist attacks.

As Christians, how do we face fear? Phillip Keller writes, "Too many of us are shaken up, frightened and panicked by the storms of life. We claim to have confidence in Christ but when the first dark shadows sweep over us and the path we tread looks gloomy we go into a deep slump of despair. . . . This is not as it should be."[29]

When fear invades our spirits, we need to turn to the One in whom we have confidence—Jesus Christ, the Good Shepherd. The One who tells us that He is with us always, "to the very end of the age" (Matthew 28:20 NIV).

Oswald Chambers writes, "The problems of life get hold of a man or woman and make it difficult to know whether in the face of these things he or she really is confident in Jesus Christ. The attitude of a believer must be 'Things do look bad, but I believe Him; and when the whole thing is told I am confident my belief will be justified and God will be revealed as a God of love and justice.' It does not mean that we won't have problems, but it does mean that our problems will never come in between us and our faith in Him. 'Lord, I don't understand this, but I am certain that there will be an explanation, and in the meantime I put it to one side.'"[30]

Although we may not understand why certain things happen in our lives, God instructs us to be strong and courageous, for "no one will be able to stand up against you all the days of your life. . . . I will be with you; I will never leave you nor forsake you" (Joshua 1:5 NIV). Do you have this confidence—that God is with you in the storms of life? That you can trust in Him and He will bring you through it all? Or do you trust in something other than Christ: "Some trust in chariots and some in horses, but we trust in the name of the LORD our God" (Psalm 20:7 NIV).

David wrote of his trust in God in many of the Psalms, most notably, Psalm 23: "I will fear no evil, for you are with me" (verse 4 NIV). Phillip Keller writes, "It is a most reassuring and reinforcing experience to the child of God to discover that there is, even in the dark valley, a source of strength and courage to be found in God. . . . Because He has led me through without fear before, He can do it again, and again, and again. In this knowledge fear fades and tranquility of heart and mind takes its place."[31]

The only confidence we have in this life is knowing that God is always with us. He is our Protector, Comforter, and Guide. And if we are wise enough, we will look for and find God in every moment, filled with the assurance that He is with us through the good and the bad, the known and the unknown, the beginning and the end. He is there when others are not. If we follow God—through prayer and the reading and application of His Word—He will keep us close to Him, traveling down the right path, until we reach our home, where He greets us. Within the shelter of His embrace, fear is vanquished.

Phillip Keller writes, "The person with a powerful confidence in Christ; the one who has proved by past experience that God is with him in adversity; the one who walks through life's dark valleys without fear, his head held high, is the one who in turn is a tower of strength and a source of inspiration to his companions."[32]

Be a person with powerful confidence in Christ. Renew your mind each and every morning with God's truth, for that truth is what will keep you confident and expectant throughout the day. Plant God's Word in your heart and mind. Pray for His deliverance: "Deliver me from evil." Leave your fears at His feet.

Reflect on your past experiences, how God has carried you through. Go to your Protector, Guide, and Good Shepherd, for He and His Word are the only things that can set you free from all fear as You trust and hope in Him. Know that "God will command his angels to protect you wherever you go. They will carry you in their arms, and you won't hurt your feet on the stones" (Psalm 91:11–12 CEV).

I arise today, through. . .
God's host to save me.

A Prayer for Deliverance

I sought the LORD, and He heard me, and delivered me from all my fears.
PSALM 34:4 NKJV

I am here, seeking You, Lord. I am looking in Your Word for courage and strength. Help me to have more confidence in You. You are my rock and my refuge. Bring me up to where You are. I want to commune with You, to rest with You, to be head over heels "in trust" with You. Show me how to do that, Lord. As I look upon Your face, deliver me from this burden of fear. I long to dwell in Your presence here and now, and when I rise from this place of prayer, I long to take You with me through my day. You are my courage and my strength. Nothing can harm me.

Never Alone

"I will never leave you nor forsake you."
JOSHUA 1:5 NIV

*Y*our Word says that You will never leave me, but right now I feel all alone. I am afraid of what lies before me. Help me to know, beyond a shadow of a doubt, that You are with me. You are my Good Shepherd. With You by my side, I need not fear. Fill me with Your presence and Your courage as I greet this day.

Calling All Angels

God will command his angels to protect you wherever you go. They will carry you in their arms, and you won't hurt your feet on the stones.
PSALM 91:11–12 CEV

*O*h, what a tremendous God You are! You have commanded Your angels to surround me. Right now they are protecting me, guarding me from danger. You will not let anything that is not of Your will touch me. You won't even let me trip over a stone. With Your heavenly host surrounding me, there is no need to fear. Still my rapidly beating heart as I take one breath. . .then another. . .then another, here in Your presence. You are an awesome God. You are *my* God. Thank You for always being there—here—in my heart.

Calm My Heart

God has not given us a spirit of timidity, but of power and love and discipline.
2 TIMOTHY 1:7 NASB

*L*ord, rid me of the fears that are plaguing me as I come to You this morning. Calm my racing heart. Fill me with Your strength and courage. The storms, the trials, feel as if they are going to overcome me, but You have overcome the world and will not let me be brought down. You have given me the spirit of power, love, and self-discipline, and I revel in this knowledge. I praise Your name, Your saving name!

Worldly Fears

"But blessed is the man who trusts in the LORD, whose confidence is in him."
JEREMIAH 17:7 NIV

I am so blessed for even though I fear many things right now—the state of the economy, unemployment, terrorist attacks, shootings in the schools and on the streets, lack of health care coverage—I trust in You. I refuse to go along with the world, driven by despair, fear, and insecurity. No, I will not bow to outside pressures. I will live my life with the assurance that You are with me. I will put my confidence in You, for I trust You to look out for me, to keep me close to You, to always be with me, no matter what.

One Way Out

Trust in the LORD with all your heart and lean not on your own understanding;
in all your ways acknowledge him, and he will make your paths straight.
PROVERBS 3:5–6 NIV

*L*ord, I am so afraid of what this day may bring. So many times I have tried to make this situation right and nothing seems to be working. I cannot figure a way out anymore. Help me to trust in You—not just halfway but the whole way. I don't understand what's happening, but I acknowledge Your presence in my life and Your ability to make all things right.

Fear of the Future

I rise early, before the sun is up; I cry out for help and put my hope in your words.
PSALM 119:147 NLT

*H*ere I am, Lord, rising before the dawn, crying to You for help for that is the desperate state I am in. I fear what this day may bring, or if not this day, the next. Your Word is the only relief, the only confidence, the only rock on which I can stand. Strengthen me with Your courage. You said You would never leave me nor forsake me. So come to me now. Rise within my spirit. Lift me up to the Rock that is higher than I. I want to soar like an eagle and fly into Your arms where I know I will be safe, protected, and loved. Keep Your hand upon me this day and all my days.

In God I Trust

But even when I am afraid, I keep on trusting you. I praise your promises!
I trust you and am not afraid. No one can harm me.
PSALM 56:3–4 CEV

*W*hen all is said and done, it simply comes down to this, Lord: In whom do I trust? If I allow messages from the devil to fill my mind, I will be defeated. You have overcome this world, You have overcome the evil one. Plant Your Word in my mind so that there is no room for the fears that threaten to consume me. Help me to remember that I need never fear, for You are with me.

Protection from Evil

My victory and honor come from God alone. He is my refuge, a rock where no
enemy can reach me. O my people, trust in him at all times.
Pour out your heart to him, for God is our refuge.
PSALM 62:7–8 NLT

*I*t is well with my soul, for I am Your child and You protect me
from all evils. I come to You, pouring out my heart, sharing my
fears and worries. Take these fears from me and shepherd me
to a place close beside You. Snuggle up close to me and fill me
with the comfort of Your Word. Help me to be still and listen
to Your advice. I want to know what You want me to do. Dispel
the negative thoughts and fill me with Your Word, for that is the
power that will get me through this day and the days to come.

Strength and Courage in Hope

Be of good courage, and He shall strengthen your heart, all you who hope in the LORD.
PSALM 31:24 NKJV

*E*ach and every day, just like today, I arise in the morning,
afraid of what the day may bring. But then I remember You,
and I come to You in prayer. Your Word brings me light. Your
presence brings me comfort. I breathe in Your strength and
exhale my fears. Strength in. . .fears out. I have courage of
spirit and strength of heart for all my hope—today and every
day—is in You and You alone.

No Man Can Harm Me

So we say with confidence, "The Lord is my helper;
I will not be afraid. What can man do to me?"
HEBREWS 13:6 NIV

*W*ow! I claim this promise for myself today, Lord. I commit it to memory. You are my Helper and I will *not* be afraid—of anything! You are my Helper, my Rock, my Refuge. You'll shield me from any and all troubles this world can throw at me. I feel You sitting beside me, Your hands upon mine. Nothing can harm me with You by my side. How awesome is that! Today, I arise with confidence, telling the whole world, "The Lord is my Helper! I am not afraid!"

Prayer for Protection

So do not throw away your confidence; it will be richly rewarded. . . . But we are not of
those who shrink back and are destroyed, but of those who believe and are saved.
HEBREWS 10:35, 39 NIV

*L*ord, help me to be a frugal Christian and not throw away my confidence in You. Fill my spirit with power and courage so I can face this day with You beside me, ready to protect me at a moment's notice. I believe in You. You will save me, bringing me through the fire and flood, the storm and desert. You are holding my hand, shielding me from the evils of this world. Thank You, Lord, for walking with me through the shadows of this valley.

Fear of My Enemies

I will call upon the LORD, who is worthy to be praised; so shall I be saved from my enemies. . . . For by You I can run against a troop, by my God I can leap over a wall. . . . As for God, His way is perfect; the word of the LORD is proven; He is a shield to all who trust in Him.

PSALM 18:3, 29–30 NKJV

*T*oday, Lord, I feel as if my enemies are surrounding me and there is no way out. But that is wrong thinking, wrong feeling. That is not the truth of the situation. The truth is that with You, nothing is impossible. With You, I can do anything, even leap over a wall. There is nothing to fear. Your way is perfect and Your Word, on which I totally rely, is filled with promises made and kept. Today I face my enemies and stand with You, surrounded by Your shield on each and every side. I take my refuge in You.

Leaning on the Word

For you have been my hope, O Sovereign LORD, my confidence since my youth.

PSALM 71:5 NIV

*L*ord, since I've known You, You have been my hope—most times my only hope. You give me confidence to face the day. Sometimes I'm afraid to step out the door, to watch the news, to read the paper. But at those times all I need to do is remember Your Word and trust in that. Your Word is my confidence and my strength. When those arrows of misfortune come my way, help me to lean back and rest in Your Word, committing Your promises to memory, strengthening my spirit and my soul.

My To-Do List

The Power of Walking with God

It is God who works in you both to will and to do for His good pleasure.
PHILIPPIANS 2:13 NKJV

*I*n centuries past, the age-old question was "To be or not to be?" Today it's "To do or not to do?" Armed with lists of tasks to accomplish at work, home, and church, we spend our days running at breakneck speed, trying desperately to cross off each item from a list that seemingly never ends.

Bill Hybels writes, "The archenemy of spiritual authenticity is busyness which is closely tied to something the Bible calls worldliness—getting caught up with this society's agenda, objectives and activities to the neglect of walking with God."[33]

We are called to *"Be* still, and know that I am God" (Psalm 46:10 NKJV, emphasis added). But when we are caught up in society's frenzied pace, our seemingly endless to-do list threatens to crowd out our time "to be"—with God, our spouse, our children, our friends. So how do we decide every day what God wants us to do? And how can we prevent our frantic quest of *doing* from stealing our joy of *being*?

First, every morning go to God for renewal and edification. He will give you the energy to do whatever needs to be done. "He energizes those who get tired. . . . Those who wait upon

GOD get fresh strength" (Isaiah 40:29, 31 THE MESSAGE). And as He is refreshing and energizing you, He's listening. Present your to-do lists for His input. There may be things He'd like to add or things He is prompting you to do, such as spending an intimate evening with your spouse, calling an old acquaintance, or visiting a housebound relative. Allow God to reorient your priorities in light of Romans 12:2—"Don't be like the people of this world, but let God change the way you think. Then you will know how *to do* everything that is good and pleasing to him" (CEV, emphasis added).

Second, realize your limits. You may not get everything done in one day. Take a look at the tasks listed and, if necessary, pare them down to a manageable number. Sometimes it's necessary to allow others to help share the load you bear. John Wesley said, "Though I am always in haste, I am never in a hurry, because I never undertake more work than I can go through with calmness of spirit." Ask God for guidance in what not "to do."

Third, be wise in the things you choose to do. Gordon MacDonald writes, "One of the great tests of human character is found in making critical choices of selection and rejection amidst all of the opportunities that lurk in life's path. . . . Sometimes. . .I had to say no to things I really wanted to do in order to say yes to the very best things."[34] Don't try to be a people pleaser by saying yes to things you really don't have time for. Instead, prayerfully consider the opportunity before you and, when necessary, "Just say no."

Fourth, leave time in your schedule for the unexpected, like giving your son a ride to school when he misses his bus. Instead of being frustrated about this interruption in your schedule, turn your attention and love to the child sitting next to you in the car. It's more important that you be with him or her than getting your laundry done today. Rest easy in those unexpected moments together.

Fifth, spend time *being* as you're *doing*. Throughout the activities of your day, be the child God wants you to be, one filled with love and joy, one who is patient, forgiving, and kind, calm, unhurried, anxious about nothing. Take time to smell the coffee, to look around at God's wonders, to just *be*.

Sixth, *make sure you have your priorities straight*. Your spiritual and physical health comes first. Next are your spouse and family, followed by your relationships with people at church, work, community, and play. Make sure *things* don't crowd out *people*.

When we review our to-do lists with our priorities clearly outlined before us and God in the forefront of our minds, we are reorienting our lives to please God, ensuring that our days will be spent walking in His path as we accomplish our daily tasks. Come to God each morning. Spend time at His feet, dwelling on His truths. Examine yesterday's happenings and present today's tasks. Ask Him what He wants you to do. Then you will yield the fruit He wants you to yield (see Psalm 1:2–3). Above all, don't get caught up in the busyness of this life (see Luke 8:14). Instead, allow Jesus to refocus your priorities, and be firm in the belief that no matter what happens today, " 'God is with you in all that you do' " (Genesis 21:22 NKJV).

Christ with me.

Overwhelmed

For we are His workmanship, created in Christ Jesus for good works, which God prepared beforehand that we should walk in them.

EPHESIANS 2:10 NKJV

*G*od, I have so many things to do today. I feel overwhelmed. But I am here to be Your hands and feet. You have known since the beginning of time what I am to accomplish each and every day. Give me the wisdom to do what You want me to do, to be the person You want me to be.

Renew My Strength

He gives power to the weak, and to those who have no might He increases strength. . . . Those who wait on the LORD shall renew their strength; they shall mount up with wings like eagles, they shall run and not be weary, they shall walk and not faint.

ISAIAH 40:29, 31 NKJV

I didn't get half the things I needed to do accomplished yesterday, Lord. And today I feel as if I have no energy. I am flagging, Lord, and I don't know what to do. So I arise early and come here to spend time with You. Calm my nerves. Remind me that the world is not going to fall apart if I don't accomplish everything on my to-do list today or even tomorrow, yet show me how to use my time wisely. Give my heart peace, and as I spend these moments with You, give me strength so that I may walk in Your power.

Let It Be

Trust in the LORD with all your heart, and lean not on your own understanding; in all your ways acknowledge Him, and He shall direct your paths.

PROVERBS 3:5–6 NKJV

I acknowledge that You are in control of everything, Lord, and that the things You want me to accomplish today will get done. I want to walk in Your will and not in mine. I want to lean on Your Word and take Your paths. I can only do that by putting my total trust in You as I go through this day. I want to be like Mary. I want to be Your servant, saying, " 'Let it be to me according to your word' " (Luke 1:38 NKJV). So, Lord, help me to accomplish want You want me to do today, and let the rest be.

Change My Thoughts

Don't be like the people of this world, but let God change the way you think. Then you will know how to do everything that is good and pleasing to him.

ROMANS 12:2 CEV

*L*ord, I don't want to be like the people of this world, running around at breakneck speed, trying to multitask until I'm so deep in the darkness I can no longer see the light of Your face. It's not all about doing; it's about being. Change *my* way of thinking to *Your* way of thinking. I take this to-do list and place it in Your capable hands. Help me to see this list through Your eyes. Show me clearly the steps I am to take today.

Rush Hour

Anxiety in the heart of man causes depression, but a good word makes it glad.
PROVERBS 12:25 NKJV

*H*ere I am, Lord, getting ready for another busy day, preparing myself to face rush hour. Help me to stay calm throughout this day and not get caught up in the frenzied pace of this world but to set a pace that is pleasing to You. Sure and steady wins the race, and my race is to win the prize of Your presence in my life. Help me to keep that in the forefront of my mind today. May I not become anxious but keep Your Word of peace in my heart and be a beacon of peace in the presence of others.

My Main Desire

One thing I have desired of the LORD, that will I seek: That I may dwell in the house of the LORD all the days of my life, to behold the beauty of the LORD, and to inquire in His temple.
PSALM 27:4 NKJV

*L*ord, help me to keep the main thing the main thing—and that is to seek first the kingdom of God, beholding Your beauty, inquiring in Your temple. That is all that is truly important, not whether or not I get all my work done at home, the office, or church. As I receive requests for my time and ability, give me wisdom to say yes and no in accordance with Your will.

Bearing Fruit

But his delight is in the law of the LORD, and in His law he meditates day and night. He shall be like a tree planted by the rivers of water, that brings forth its fruit in its season, whose leaf also shall not wither; and whatever he does shall prosper.

PSALM 1:2–3 NKJV

I come to You this morning, meditating on Your law, Your Word. That is my living water. You are the quencher of my thirst, You provide everything for me. Because of Your presence in my life, I can bring forth the fruit You want me to bear. As I go through the activities of this day, may Your hand be upon me so that whatever I do will prosper. To Your good and great glory, Lord, amen!

Keeping Priorities Straight

"God is with you in all that you do."
GENESIS 21:22 NKJV

*L*ord, as I go through this day, help me to keep my priorities straight. It's not all about what I do but how I treat others. Show me how to love those I come in contact with as I go through my daily routine and run my errands. Help me be a person of compassion. When people see me, I want them to recognize You, because that's what the world needs more of these days—Your love, Your face, Your presence, Your light.

Capturing Thoughts

We are taking every thought captive to the obedience of Christ.
2 CORINTHIANS 10:5 NASB

*G*od, it seems like I need a reminder every moment of the day to listen to Your voice. I keep getting caught up in the world of busyness and that's not where You want me to be. Help me not to be overwhelmed by the demands of this society but to be open to Your voice. I want to hear You speak to me all throughout the day. I want to do only what You want me to do each moment. Remind me to take each thought captive to Christ so that I am not misled, going somewhere or doing something that is not of You.

No Worries

"The seed which fell among the thorns, these are the ones who have heard, and as they go on their way they are choked with worries and riches and pleasures of this life, and bring no fruit to maturity."
LUKE 8:14 NASB

I'm not letting the worries of this day get me away from You, Lord. I'll not go out into the world seeking gold—a temporary blessing at best—but You and Your will. I seek first Your presence as I come to You in prayer. I lay myself before You, Your willing servant. May everything I do today leave Your fingerprints, because that is why You created me. Help me to be a blessing to all those I meet.

Peace amid Interruptions

We continually remember before our God and Father your work produced by faith, your labor prompted by love, and your endurance inspired by hope in our Lord Jesus Christ.

1 Thessalonians 1:3 niv

*H*ere I am, Lord, ready to receive my marching orders for today. Arm me with faith, love, and hope. I am strong in You. I expect You to be with me all through the day. There is nothing that can frustrate me when I remain in Your presence. With every interruption, I am calm and accepting, because the prince of this world, the evil one, is unable to steal my peace and joy. For You, my Lord and Savior, have overcome this world! Hallelujah!

Lead Me by the Hand

A man's heart plans his way, but the Lord directs his steps.

Proverbs 16:9 nkjv

*H*ere we go, Lord—another morning with a thousand things to do. Lead me by the hand, for I don't know which way to go. I have trouble with my priorities, Lord. The only thing I seem to be able to remember is that You are first in all things. So here I am, seeking You first. Plan my day as You see fit. Direct my steps to walk Your path. Life can get so complicated, Lord, so help me to keep it simple, remembering that You are working in me both to will and to do for Your pleasure.

With Him Each Moment

"But more than anything else, put God's work first and do what he wants.
Then the other things will be yours as well."
MATTHEW 6:33 CEV

I can't seem to find any time, Lord. It's always rush, rush, rush. I need to remember that I am already with You in the heavenlies. Calm my heart. Help me to breathe slower. I want to relax here at Your feet. I want to smell Your perfume, touch Your robe, hear Your voice. When I do Your work today, everything else will then fall into place. I lean back against Your knees, waiting to hear Your voice.

God's Glory, not Mine

Whatever you do, do all to the glory of God.
1 CORINTHIANS 10:31 NASB

*I*t's all for You, Lord, everything I do today. I refuse to get caught up in the mad rush. I refuse to seek only temporal satisfaction. I am here to please You and You only. Help me not to stretch myself so thin that I am unable to do the things You want me to do. I am here for You and for You alone. Give me the energy I need to accomplish those tasks for Your glory. And tonight may You say, "Ah, my good and faithful servant, well done!"

My Blessings

The Power of Assurance

I will bless you [with abundant increase of favors]...
and you will be a blessing [dispensing good to others].
GENESIS 12:2 AMP

*T*he Bible is full of God's blessings for our lives, full of positive words, promises granted to those who choose to follow Him, who choose to believe in His assurances. Hebrews 11:8 tells us that "by faith Abraham obeyed when he was called to go out to the place which he would receive as an inheritance" and that "he went out, not knowing where he was going" (NKJV). And when Abraham arrived at his destination, God *met him there* and gave him a brand-new promise: "I will bless you...and you will be a blessing" (Genesis 12:2 AMP). As sons and daughters of Abraham (see Galatians 3:7), we share in this promise! We can be filled with assurance that wherever we go, God will bless us. He is even going before us, ready to greet us with a word of encouragement when we get there.

Is your faith strong enough and your mind open enough to make room for God's bounty of blessings? Or is your faith too little, your mind too closed? Perhaps you feel you are undeserving. If so, plant the words of Hebrews 11:6 in your heart: "Without faith it is impossible to please and be satisfactory to Him. For whoever would come near to God must [necessarily] believe that God exists and that He is the rewarder of those who earnestly and diligently seek Him [out]" (AMP). Claim the promise of 1 John 5:14–15: "Now this is the confidence that we have in Him, that if we ask anything according to His will, He hears us. And if we know that He hears us, whatever we ask, we know that we have the petitions that we have asked of Him" (NKJV). It's not a matter of deserving but of firm faith, great expectation, and sincere seeking.

Don't buy into the negative mindset of the spies in Numbers 13:33, who were not willing to take possession of the land that God had promised them. Adopt the firm stance of Caleb and Joshua: "[God] will bring us into this land and give it to us, a land flowing with milk and honey" (Numbers 14:8 AMP). Believe God's promise of bounty: " 'And try Me now in this,' says the LORD of hosts, 'If I will not open for you the windows of heaven and pour out for you such blessing that there will not be room enough to receive it' " (Malachi 3:10 NKJV). Drop your doubt and disbelief, let go of negative thinking, and make room in your arms to receive God's blessings.

Thank God for eternal promises, past blessings, and the assurance of blessings to come. By doing so, you'll avoid the pitfall of seeing the world through eyes of discouragement. Andrew Murray writes, "The faith that always thanks Him— not for experiences, but for the promises on which it can rely—goes on from strength to strength, still increasing in the blessed assurance that God Himself will perfect His work in us."[35] Praise and thank God for all His blessings, focusing on the Giver and not on the gift.

Remember that this promise of blessing works two ways. We are blessed *and* we are *to be* a blessing to others. Job consistently blessed the lives of others, saying that if he had not, "then let my arm fall from my shoulder, let my arm be torn from the socket" (Job 31:22 NKJV). Are *you* that consistent in your bestowal of blessings? First Peter 3:9 says, "Bless—that's your job, to bless. You'll be a blessing and also get a blessing" (THE MESSAGE). The law of sowing and reaping ensures us that as you sow blessings, you will reap much of the same. But how do you find out whom or how God wants you to bless?

Go to God and ask Him to plant a seed in your mind, giving you specific ways to bless others in specific instances. Spend some quiet moments in His presence, listening for His direction. Then make sure you do what He tells you. For a general idea of how to be a blessing to everyone, consider 1 Peter 3:10–12: "Whoever wants to embrace life and see the day fill up with good, here's what you do: Say nothing evil or hurtful; snub evil and cultivate good; run after peace for all you're worth. God looks on all this with approval, listening and responding well to what he's asked" (THE MESSAGE).

During your quiet time, make a list of how the Lord has blessed you in the past. Then make a list of the blessings you anticipate in the present and the future. Don't buy into a negative mindset. Believe that God has good things out there just waiting for you to open your arms to receive them. Empty yourself of disbelief and discouragement. Revel in the power of assurance that God is ready and willing to bless your life. And be sure to pray for an opportunity to be a blessing to others.

Choose to believe that Christ loves you and is blessing you even in the midst of trials. He always goes before you, planting blessings on your path. God is One who "daily loads us with benefits" (Psalm 68:19 NKJV). Your job: Claim them today.

Christ before me.

Sharing My Blessings

"Every man shall give as he is able, according to the blessing of the
LORD your God which He has given you."
DEUTERONOMY 16:17 NASB

*L*ord, You have blessed me and the works of my hands. I am so grateful to You for all that I have. As You bless me, I am able to bless others in whatever way I can. What a feeling to know that I am able to help expand Your kingdom! Help me to tithe my talents, monies, and time, all to Your glory. For Thine is the kingdom and the power, forever and ever.

Obedience and Blessings

All these blessings will come down on you and spread out beyond you
because you have responded to the Voice of GOD, your God.
DEUTERONOMY 28:2 THE MESSAGE

I hear Your voice, Lord, and I thank You for the blessings that You have showered upon me. Sometimes I feel so unworthy, but You love me so much that at times I cannot understand it. All that You have blessed me with goes beyond me, as I respond to Your voice, do Your will, and work to serve others. Speak to me, Lord. Tell me whom, what, and where You want me to bless. I am Your servant, Lord; speak to me.

Guaranteed Blessing

"The Lord will guarantee a blessing on everything you do."
DEUTERONOMY 28:8 NLT

Your Word says that You actually *guarantee* a blessing on everything I do! That's a promise I can count on, and one I revel in. It gives me the confidence that You will be with me in all that I do, blessing me at each and every turn. What an awesome promise! I arise today, assured of Your assistance, guidance, and approval of every good thing. There are no words to express how You make me feel. I am humbled in Your presence and renewed in Your light. I praise You, Lord!

Choosing Life

"I call heaven and earth as witnesses today against you, that I have set before you life and death, blessing and cursing; therefore choose life, that both you and your descendants may live."
DEUTERONOMY 30:19 NKJV

Lord, this day I choose life—I choose to live and work and have my being in You. Instead of looking at all that I don't have, I choose to look at all that You have blessed me with—family, friends, a home, a job, clothes on my back, food in my belly. . . . Oh Lord, the list is endless. Thank You so much for being my life, today and every day! I cling to You, each and every moment. Live through me!

An Awesome God

God's blessing makes life rich; nothing we do can improve on God.
PROVERBS 10:22 THE MESSAGE

*I*t is Your presence, Your blessings, Your love that makes my life so rich and fulfilling. I am not worried about what others have and I have not. I am full of joy for what I do have—mainly You! There is nothing greater than You, Lord. You are an awesome God. Nothing I do can make You any greater than Your word and Your promises. I praise You for what You are doing in my life, for making me rich beyond my wildest dreams as I live and breathe in You.

Daily Benefits

Blessed be the Lord, who daily loads us with benefits, the God of our salvation!
PSALM 68:19 NKJV

I am loaded with benefits! Blessed beyond compare! You, the God of my salvation, the Friend who laid down His life for me, the One who is with me in fire, flood, and famine, the One who will never leave me or forsake me! Today is a new day, and You have benefits waiting out there for me. I begin the day in my walk toward You, leaving my burdens behind and focusing on the benefits ahead. And when I come to You at the close of the day, You will be waiting for me, at the end of the path, with a good word.

The Right Focus

"For I will pour out water to quench your thirst and to irrigate your parched fields. And I will pour out my Spirit on your descendants, and my blessing on your children."

ISAIAH 44:3 NLT

*L*ord, I am thirsty, parched with the demands of this world. I am in want in so many ways. Help me not to focus on what I don't have, but to focus on You and the blessings that You have prepared for me and my children. Pour out Your Spirit upon me now. Fill me with Your presence. Give me hope for this day. I anticipate blessings waiting around every corner. Thank You, Lord, for taking such good care of me. You, my Savior, are the greatest blessing of all!

A Symbol and Source of Blessing

"Now I will rescue you and make you both a symbol and a source of blessing. So don't be afraid. Be strong."

ZECHARIAH 8:13 NLT

*L*ord, Your Son has already rescued me! I am so full of joy! You have made me both a symbol of that blessing and a source of blessing to others. I am not afraid of things in this world for I am assured of Your promises. I will be strong, confident in the benefits You bestow upon me, able to stretch myself as I strive to reach others so that they, too, will have the benefit of Your blessings. What power! What confidence! What hope!

The Law of Sowing and Reaping

"Bring your full tithe to the Temple treasury so there will be ample provisions
in my Temple. Test me in this and see if I don't open up heaven itself to you
and pour out blessings beyond your wildest dreams."
MALACHI 3:10 THE MESSAGE

*L*ord, Your Word says it is true—the more I give, the more I get. Yet that's not why I do it. I give of myself to bless others because that is what You have called me to do. The more I step out in Your Word, with You walking before me, the more I am blessed by Your presence and Your promises. It's not all about material things, although those are blessings as well. But I am more focused on the spiritual, for that is what keeps me close to You, unshaken, undisturbed, unfettered. Praise be Your holy name!

Heavenly Blessings

All praise to God, the Father of our Lord Jesus Christ, who has blessed us with every
spiritual blessing in the heavenly realms because we are united with Christ.
EPHESIANS 1:3 NLT

*B*ecause I am united with Your Son, who gave His life so that we could live, You have blessed me with every spiritual blessing. Here I sit, at my Savior's knee, His hand upon my head. I am at peace. I am blessed. I am in the heavenly realms. Here, nothing can harm me, for He has blessed me beyond measure. Lord, my cup runneth over with love for You!

My Job

Bless — that's your job, to bless. You'll be a blessing and also get a blessing.
1 PETER 3:9 THE MESSAGE

*M*y job—to bless others. What an awesome privilege to be an extension of Your arm. To bless others, who don't even know I am the blesser! That's so cool. To do these things in secret, not wanting to be known, fills me with so much pleasure. There is nothing like it. Show me whose lives I can bless today, even in the simplest of things.

Blessing Enemies

Bless those who persecute you [who are cruel in their attitude toward you];
bless and do not curse them.
ROMANS 12:14 AMP

*G*od, I pray that You will bless those who have not been kind to me. You know who they are. Give me the blessing of forgiving others as You always forgive me. Help me not to repay evil with evil, but to repay evil with good, for that is what You would have me do. Give me the strength to be kind to them, even helpful, and to keep my anger and frustration at bay. Bless their lives, Lord. In Jesus' name I pray.

Praise Ye the Lord

May the peoples praise you, O God; may all the peoples praise you. Then the land will yield its harvest, and God, our God, will bless us.

PSALM 67:5–6 NIV

I praise God from whom all blessings flow. You bless us beyond measure, we the sheep of Your pasture. You give us green meadows in which to lie down, calm waters to give us rest. You forgive us our sins. You love us beyond measure. There is no greater blessing than Your presence in my life, than Your desire to hear of all my troubles, cares, and woes. You are here to lift the burden from my shoulders and shower blessings down upon me. I praise the name of Jesus in whom I cannot but trust.

A Daily Benediction

"'The LORD bless you, and keep you; the LORD make His face shine on you, and be gracious to you; the LORD lift up His countenance on you, and give you peace.'"

NUMBERS 6:24–26 NASB

*M*ay You walk down the road with me today. May You shower my path with Your many blessings. May You keep me from danger. May Your light keep me from the darkness surrounding me. May You give me grace and peace and strength for the day. May You give me someone to bless as You have blessed me. May You be there, waiting for me, at the end of the day, with a good word to calm my spirit as I rest in Your arms.

My Finances

The Power of Contentment

True godliness with contentment is itself great wealth.
1 TIMOTHY 6:6 NLT

God wants us to be content—physically, emotionally, and financially—no matter what our circumstances. This can be a challenge for those of us who live in a society driven by the need to be one step ahead of the Joneses. But as Christians we must live by the maxim that it's not all about the money—it's all about God.

Money in itself is not evil. Our Creator wants us to prosper. He just doesn't want affluence to obscure our vision of living godly lives. He knows that the more we have materially, the less we will perceive a need for Him (see Deuteronomy 8:1–18). So, to prevent money and finances from being the main focus of our lives, several things must be kept in mind.

First and foremost, we are to seek God and His righteousness (see Matthew 6:33). It's okay to want to have enough money to provide for you and yours and maybe a little extra for that dream vacation. In fact, we are called to be diligent in taking care of ourselves and our family (see 1 Timothy 5:8). The problems arise when we begin loving money for itself, for *that* is the root of all evil (see 1 Timothy 6:10 KJV). Jesus said, "Ye cannot serve God and mammon" (Matthew 6:24 KJV). Make serving and worshiping the Lord your number one priority.

Second, we are to be wise in the spending of money. Our constant pursuit of the latest gadget can easily lead us into debt and perhaps financial ruin. I don't know how many times I've been swayed by advertisers who tell me that I can lose ten pounds in two weeks just by using their latest piece of exercise equipment. The before-and-after pictures of those who have are amazing. How could I *not* lose? And if I hurry now, I won't have to pay full price. What a deal! As I reach for the phone, my finger poised to dial the 1-800 number, where operators are just waiting to take my call, the Spirit prompts me to think again. In obedience, I send up a question to God: "Lord, do You think purchasing this item is a good idea for me at this time?" If the answer is unclear, I give myself a few more days to think about it. Nine times out of ten, I soon forget about the whole thing. We need to guard against the plethora of advertising ploys out there. Ask yourself and God, "Is this item truly necessary?"

Third, we are to be content with what we have. This truism is covered not only in 1 Timothy 6:6 but also in two of the Ten Commandments, where God tells us neither to steal nor to covet our neighbor's possessions (see Exodus 20:15, 17). When we find ourselves discontent with what we have, we are "greedy for gain," which "takes away the life of its owners" (Proverbs 1:19 NKJV).

Fourth, we cannot allow money worries to steal our joy. Remember the words of Jesus, who told us to be anxious for nothing (see Matthew 6:25–32). Rest in the assurance that God cares about us and will see to our every need.

Fifth, be ever mindful that what we have isn't ours but God's. " 'The earth and everything in it belong to the Lord' " (1 Corinthians 10:26 CEV). All God has made—you, your children, your spouse, your possessions—is His (see Job 41:11 NKJV)! We are mere stewards of God's possessions during our time on earth. Although we can and should enjoy everything He has put under our care, we are never to forget that all we have is to be used to extend *His* kingdom, not ours.

Sixth, we are to be givers to God. When we get our paycheck, we should readily give God His portion, for in kingdom-of-God reality the money is all His to begin with. Donald Whitney writes, "So the question is not, 'How much of my money should I give to God?' but rather, 'How much of God's money should I keep for myself?' "[36]

Seventh, do not "trust in uncertain riches but in the living God, who gives us richly all things to enjoy" (1 Timothy 6:17 NKJV). Don't put all your faith in the temporal blessings— money and possessions that will one day be eaten away by moths and rust—but have confidence in the One who *provides* those blessings. Simply live each day trusting in God, and He will bless your life (see Jeremiah 17:7).

Finally, give up extraneous possessions whenever possible. Think of all the time you spend taking care of your temporal goods. So much time, perhaps, that you may feel as if your possessions own you. If that's the case, perhaps you should empty your arms so that you'll have room for future blessings. Begin by looking around the room you're in right now. Ask God what you should give away to someone in need and then do so. Remember that "caring for the poor is lending to the LORD, and you will be well repaid" (Proverbs 19:17 CEV).

Take charge of your finances but don't let them take charge of you, and whenever possible, don't charge at all. Simply live your life by seeking God first, not earthly treasures. Then and only then will you be blessed and prosper. Tap into the power of contentment, making Christ your financial backer.

Christ behind me.

Learned Contentment

I have learned, in whatsoever state I am, therewith to be content.
PHILIPPIANS 4:11 KJV

*L*ord, I am so happy just as I am. There is nothing better than being in Your presence, seeking Your face. I thank You for all my blessings, in good times and bad. I thank You for Your Son, who died on the cross so that I could live forever. I thank You for Your Word and the treasures I find there. I go forth in this day, with the power of contentment firmly in my heart. Lead me where You will. I am ready to follow.

Strength for the Work Ahead

If you start thinking to yourselves, "I did all this. And all by myself. I'm rich. It's all mine!"—well, think again. Remember that GOD, your God, gave you the strength to produce all this wealth so as to confirm the covenant that he promised to your ancestors—as it is today.
DEUTERONOMY 8:18 THE MESSAGE

*Y*ou promised to bless me and mine. I thank You for all the spiritual, physical, and financial gifts You have showered upon me. You give me the physical strength to go out each and every day to work and support myself and my family. Your Word gives me the spiritual strength to battle the schemes that the evil one throws into my path. Thank You for hearing my prayers, morning after morning, strengthening me for the work ahead.

Steady Work

The one who stays on the job has food on the table; the witless chase whims and fancies.
PROVERBS 12:11 THE MESSAGE

*L*ord, show me how to be content with my job. I know I need to work diligently so that I can provide for my family but I am not sure that this is what You have called me to do. I feel trapped. Would chasing after my dream job be Your will for me or is it just a whim? Lead me in the way I should go. Help me to be content in my present job and with the money I am earning. But if it be Your will, give me the courage to pursue the dreams You have for me.

Firstfruits for God

Honor the LORD with your wealth and with the firstfruits of all your produce; then your barns will be filled with plenty, and your vats will be bursting with wine.
PROVERBS 3:9–10 ESV

*A*nother paycheck! Thank You, God, for giving me the strength to work each day. Thank You for the money I hold in my hand. Help me to remember that this is not my money, but Yours. I come to You this morning, asking You to tell me how much You want me to give to You and, if so directed, others. I want to bless Your church, Your ministries, Your people, as You have so richly blessed me. Tell me, Lord, what You would have me give away, and I will do so knowing that You will bless me.

The Power of Contentment

But godliness with contentment is great gain. For we brought nothing into this world,
and it is certain we can carry nothing out. And having food and raiment
let us be therewith content.
1 TIMOTHY 6:6–8 KJV

*O*h Lord, I feel as if I have it all. With You in my life, I need not worry about anything. For as You dress the flowers that neither toil nor spin and feed the birds that neither sow nor reap, You shall do even more for me. I do not worry about what I will eat, wear, drink, or earn today. I leave all my concerns in Your hands, knowing that You will provide. You are first in my life.

Love of Money

For the love of money is the root of all evil: which while some coveted after, they have
erred from the faith, and pierced themselves through with many sorrows.
But thou, O man of God, flee these things; and follow after righteousness,
godliness, faith, love, patience, meekness.
1 TIMOTHY 6:10–11 KJV

*D*ear God, I come to You this morning with a heavy heart. I feel as if I have let my quest for financial security take my eyes off of You. Help me to put aside my fear of never having enough and replace it with trust in You. Take away my seemingly insatiable appetite for more and more gain and replace it with the power of contentment. Free me from the snare of greed and lead me into greater faith in You.

Hope in God, Rich in Generosity

As for the rich in this present age, charge them not to be haughty, nor to set their hopes
on the uncertainty of riches, but on God, who richly provides us with everything to enjoy.
They are to do good, to be rich in good works, to be generous and ready to share, thus
storing up treasure for themselves as a good foundation for the future,
so that they may take hold of that which is truly life.

1 TIMOTHY 6:17–19 ESV

I am setting my hope on You this morning, Lord, for You provide me with everything to enjoy. Your treasure of creation— trees, flowers, children, animals, sunsets, stars—are wonders to my eyes and a balm to my heart. With You supplying all that I need, I can do good works, be ready to share, and thus build up treasures in heaven. This way of life, enveloped by Your presence, is the true way. Keep my feet sure on this path. Take care of me today and through the days to come.

God, My Treasure

If riches increase, set not your heart on them.

PSALM 62:10 ESV

*A*ll the temporal things that now surround me will one day turn to ashes and dust. They mean nothing compared to the riches I find being with You. Although things are going well now, that may not be the situation tomorrow. Thus I will not focus on what I have or do not have but on drawing ever closer to You, learning Your ways, living the life You planned for me.

Mammon Versus God

No servant can serve two masters: for either he will hate the one, and love the other; or else he will hold to the one, and despise the other. Ye cannot serve God and mammon.
LUKE 16:13 KJV

*E*verywhere I look, Lord, it seems as if everyone is chasing after money. It's no longer IN GOD WE TRUST but IN MONEY WE TRUST. And that can't be a good thing. Although I cannot control society, I can control myself. Thus this morning, I once again choose to serve You, not the almighty dollar. You are the source of all I need, of all the blessings that are awaiting me. It is in You and You alone I trust. Lift me above this obsession with material goods. I want to live in Your kingdom, not man's.

Trusting in the Lord

Blessed is the man that trusteth in the LORD, and whose hope the LORD is.
JEREMIAH 17:7 KJV

*L*ord, it is You that I trust. Not these things surrounding me, the possessions that money can buy. Those things are not alive. They are not eternal. They will never save me. Only You can do that. And when I die, these earthly things will no longer exist in my world because I will be with You in the eternal heavenlies. Thus, I will spend my life trusting in and focusing on You, knowing that You, my Good Shepherd, will take care of me, supplying all I need and more.

The True Owner

"The earth and everything in it belong to the Lord."
1 CORINTHIANS 10:26 CEV

*A*ll I have is Yours. My spouse, my children, my parents, my car, my house, my furniture—everything is Yours. Whew! Somehow that takes a load off of my mind, knowing that I am merely Your steward. Give me the wisdom, Lord, to use the things of which You have given me temporary custody to further Your kingdom. I want to live my life to Your glory, not mine. Help me to do that today. Speak to my heart, I pray.

The Right Heartset

"Did I set my heart on making big money or worship at the bank? Did I boast about my wealth, show off because I was well-off? . . . If so, I would deserve the worst of punishments, for I would be betraying God himself."
JOB 31:24–25, 28 THE MESSAGE

A heartset is like a mindset, Lord. Each morning I need to ask myself where my heart is. Is it set on making lots of money so that I can buy things I don't really need? Is my heart set on showing how much better off I am than my neighbor? Rather, I pray that my heart is set on You and what You want me to do each and every moment of the day. Help me not get caught up in this "me" world. I want my life to be all about You.

De-accumulating

Jesus said unto him, If thou wilt be perfect, go and sell that thou hast, and give to the poor, and thou shalt have treasure in heaven: and come and follow me.

MATTHEW 19:21 KJV

I want to be perfect and mature in You, Christ. I'm not sure it would be a good idea right now to sell all that I have and I'm not sure that's what You'd want. But there are things I have that I could donate to those in need. Help me not to give away the worst that I own but the best to those needing food, shelter, and clothing. Help me to choose wisely as I give to others and follow You who had nothing in this world, not even a place to lay His head, yet owned it all!

Don't Worry; Be Happy

"For this reason I say to you, do not be worried about your life, as to what you will eat or what you will drink; nor for your body, as to what you will put on. . . . For your heavenly Father knows that you need all these things."

MATTHEW 6:25, 32 NASB

*Y*our Word says I'm not to worry about my life but that seems to be all that I do. I wonder how I'm going to pay all these bills. How did I get into such a mess? Get me back on the right track, Lord. Help me to get out of debt and stay out. Help me to not worry about where the next dollar is coming from but to put all my trust in You. You know all that I need. Please, Lord, provide for me and mine.

My Friends

The Power of Encouragement

"But my mouth would encourage you;
comfort from my lips would bring you relief."
JOB 16:5 NIV

A few years ago my widowed mother ended up in the hospital. The total length of her stay was a grueling, stress-filled forty days, during which time I cared for her, conferred with her team of doctors and nurses, and juggled work, study, home, and family responsibilities.

For weeks I kept a stiff upper lip and maintained a rigid schedule, never shedding a tear. My sleep was minimal, for whenever I shut my eyes, I saw Mom lying in the hospital bed, struggling to breathe. Although I continually prayed for Mom's healing, as well as for my own strength, comfort, and guidance, the strain began to take its toll on me.

One Saturday I stayed home from the hospital to catch up on household chores. While I was vacuuming, with the vision of Mom alone in her hospital room churning through my mind, the phone rang. It was my friend and neighbor, Evelyn, asking how my mother was doing.

"Not good," I said. Tears came to the surface but I pushed them back down.

"Well," said Evelyn, 'I'm praying for you and for her. And

I'm making your family dinner tonight. What time do you want to eat? I'll bring it over."

Although my family and I hadn't had a decent home-cooked meal in weeks, I began to protest. But Evelyn insisted. Once the details were agreed upon, I hung up the phone, stunned but grateful for this simple, selfless act of kindness. I leaned on the kitchen hutch, vacuum hose in one hand, dust rag in the other, experiencing something that had been absent for the past few weeks. It was the feeling of joy and the realization that I was not alone. Suddenly, the wall crumbled and the tears began to flow. Through a simple act I was brought down to my bare emotions—and reminded of how much God cared for me through the loving-kindness of a friend.

The only thing that kept me sane during those forty days was the encouragement of my friends, expressed through their prayers, love, comfort, and service to me.

The truest earthly friends are those who share their faith in our heavenly Father. The best biblical example of friendship is that of David and Jonathan. Even though his father, King Saul, seemed determined to kill David, Jonathan told his friend, "Whatsoever thy soul desireth, I will even do it for thee" (1 Samuel 20:4 KJV). In 1 Samuel 18, we read that Jonathan "loved [David] as he loved his own soul" (verse 3 KJV; see also 1 Samuel 20:17), and then gifted him with his robe, armor, sword, bow, and belt (see verse 4). Not only did Jonathan clothe David with friendship, but he armed him as well.

In 1 Samuel, Jonathan made covenants with David (see 18:3; 20:8, 16) as well as informed him of danger (see 19:2); interceded for him (see 19:3); reconciled him to another (see 19:3–7); wept with him (see 20:41); helped to rescue him (see 20:12–13); prayed for him (see 20:13); appealed to God for him (see 20:23); and bound him to himself with promises (see 20:14–16). At their last encounter, "Jonathan. . .went to David into the wood, and strengthened his hand in God. And he said unto him, Fear not: for the hand of Saul my father shall not find thee; and thou shalt be king over Israel, and I shall be next unto thee; and that also Saul my father knoweth. And they two made a covenant before the LORD: and David abode in the wood, and Jonathan went to his house" (1 Samuel 23:16–18 KJV). Of this meeting Matthew Henry writes, "True friendship will not shrink from danger, but can easily venture, will not shrink from condescension, but can easily stoop, and exchange a palace for a wood, to serve a friend."[37] What a friendship!

Yet sometimes our friends betray or desert us. When that happens, we are to forgive them as our Father forgives us, and God will bless us for it. Larry Burkett writes, "The way Job was able to pray for his friends, even though they had already shown their true colors to him, is an indication of what kind of man he was. And, because of that, God blessed him. . . . I believe that a friend is a friend at all times (just as it says in Proverbs 17:17)."[38]

Each and every day, make it a point to encourage your friends through prayer, comfort, service, listening, and blessings. But most of all, love them, as Jonathan loved David, as Jesus loves us.

Tap into the power of encouragement and love from the greatest resource at our disposal, our greatest Friend—our one and only Savior, Jesus Christ (see John 15:15). He will never leave us nor forsake us (see Hebrews 13:5). How can He when He lives within our hearts?

Christ in me.

Consistent Love

A friend loveth at all times.
PROVERBS 17:17 KJV

*A*ll I need is love! That's all I need from my friends right now. People who care about me, who want what's best for me, who will never turn away. But when I look at my past, I wonder if *I've* always loved my friends. I mean that constant, undying, unyielding love, the kind that You show for us. Forgive me, Lord, for the times I have fallen short. For times that I was so caught up in the busyness of my day that I did not show love to a friend who really needed it. Lord, fill me and my friends with Your love, and help us to let it flow freely to all we meet.

Love One Another

[Jesus said], Love one another; as I have loved you.
JOHN 13:34 KJV

*W*hat an example of love You give us, Jesus! You laid down Your life for everyone—even while we were still sinners. Fill me with that kind of love, Lord, that self-sacrificing love. So often, my thoughts seem to be all about me and what I want. Help me to change that by following Your example. I want to be like You, serving others with compassion, understanding, patience, and kindness. Give me that power, that longing, to love those who love me, those who hate me, and those who are indifferent to me.

Turning the Other Cheek

The LORD restored the fortunes of Job when he prayed for his friends,
and the LORD increased all that Job had twofold.
JOB 42:10 NASB

*J*ob prayed for his friends even though they had showed him their true colors. That's a true friend, Lord. And when he did this, You blessed him, giving him twice as much as he had before. That's the true power of forgiveness. You know the relationships I have with my friends. Sometimes it's hard to overlook the hurtful things they say and do. Help me to be more like Job—to learn to turn the other cheek and actually serve friends who disappoint me. I ask for that kind of compassion and dedication to my friends, Lord.

Loyalty

"Is this your loyalty to your friend? Why did you not go with your friend?"
2 SAMUEL 16:17 NASB

*L*ord, I want to be a better friend to those I love. Help me to be trustworthy, devoted, and reliable. Help me to put the desires of my friends before my own. Give me the power of encouragement, so that I may be at their side with a ready word and a shoulder to lean on, with love in my heart and a prayer on my lips. I want to be like Jonathan was for David. I want to clothe others with the warmth of friendship. Make me a true friend. Whom can I help today?

Weeping with Friends

"But first, please let me spend two months, wandering in the hill country with my friends. We will cry together."

JUDGES 11:37 CEV

*L*ord, my friend is in distress. She has lost something very dear to her and she has sunk down into the abyss. Give me the power of encouragement so that I can help bear her burden. She has been there for me so many times. Now I'd like to repay that kindness, that love that she has given to me. Ease my schedule so that I can take the time out of my day to give her words of comfort. Help me lift her to You.

Forgiving Love

Beloved, let us love one another: for love is of God; and every one that loveth is born of God, and knoweth God.

1 JOHN 4:7 KJV

*Y*ou are love and You came into the world to show us that love. When we love others, we are doing what You have called us to do. But right now, Lord, I need help swallowing the resentment I feel toward my friend. She has betrayed me, and I don't know how I can love her again without Your help. This morning I pray for that forgiving love. I am saved, born of You, and I know You. Now I ask for Your love to fill me to overflowing. Help me to forgive. Heal my wounds, O Lord, my strength and song.

The Kindness of Friends

"For the despairing man there should be kindness from his friend;
so that he does not forsake the fear of the Almighty."
JOB 6:14 NASB

*L*ord, after being through this time of trial, I understand who my true friends are. Some have turned away from me, some have become indifferent to me, some no longer seek my companionship. I cannot lie. They have disappointed me. But I have also been blessed with kind friends who stick with me through thick and thin, friends who have modeled You in their lives. Thank You for those friends. May I prove myself worthy of such loyalty. And thank You, Lord, for Your eternal forgiveness and friendship. You are the One I praise!

The Help of Intercessors

"My intercessor is my friend as my eyes pour out tears to God."
JOB 16:20 NIV

I can't stop crying, Lord. So much has happened. Give me the courage to call friends, asking them to pray for me. I need their strength and encouragement. I feel so alone. I need them to help me through this, but that makes me feel weak. Yet Your Word tells me that when I am weak, You are strong. Help me to put my self-reliance aside as I seek the comfort and intercession of others. Give me courage to humble myself as I draw closer to You this morning.

Blessed with Friends

The sweet smell of incense can make you feel good, but true friendship is better still.
PROVERBS 27:9 CEV

*T*here are many wonderful things in this life, Lord. The smell of a baby's breath, the touch of a warm hand, the taste of dark chocolate—but a good word, deed, or thought from a friend is even better. There are times when I am so down. And then a friend blesses me and I think of You. It's because of You and the love that You give that makes us want to reach out to others. Thank You for blessing my life with friends.

New Friends

If you fall, your friend can help you up. But if you fall without having a friend nearby, you are really in trouble.
ECCLESIASTES 4:10 CEV

*L*ord, there are people out there that are hard to love. Help me to look beyond their cold demeanor, rudeness, shyness, negative words, and attitudes. You love each and every one of us and want us all to be friends. And if we were friends even to our enemies, the world would be at peace at last. No one deserves to be alone. Give me the courage and strength to reach out to all people and to make new friends.

Sacrificial Love

Greater love hath no man than this, that a man lay down his life for his friends.
JOHN 15:13 KJV

*W*hat a sacrifice—to lay down one's life for another! Yet that is exactly what You did for us. You allowed Yourself to be crucified and then asked God to forgive us for that dastardly deed. Oh, what a burden You bore for us. Allow me to repay You in some small way by laying my life down for my own friends. Give me the attitude of a servant, a servant like You, Jesus. Whom can I pray for and encourage today?

Building Blocks

So encourage each other and build each other up, just as you are already doing.
1 THESSALONIANS 5:11 NLT

*L*ord, I want to be a Barnabas—an encourager. I want to build people up, block by block, and not tear them down. Words can be so painful, so wrenching to the soul, heart, spirit, and confidence of others. Help me to be an encourager to others. Put a kind word in my mouth. And as I do so, may others continue to encourage me, especially those at church. Sometimes, even there, we get our feelings hurt. Help me to be Your representative, inside and outside of the body of believers. Give me words that are sweet to the soul!

Words of Encouragement

*[Jesus said,] I have called you friends; for all things that I have heard of
my Father I have made known unto you.*
JOHN 15:15 KJV

*W*hat You do for me each and every day is amazing. What
You have done for me in the past is incomprehensible. Thank
You for Your Word that shows me how great a friend You
were to me and how I can be a good friend to others as well.
There is nothing as powerful as Your Word for direction and
encouragement. This morning, this day, plant Your Word—
the elixir of life—in my heart. Mold it into my spirit. Help me
to claim it in my own life and then share it with others.

Servant Love

[Jonathan said to David,] Whatsoever thy soul desireth, I will even do it for thee.
1 SAMUEL 20:4 KJV

O Lord, I want to do whatever my friends desire, as long as it
is in accordance with Your Word. May I have the same attitude
with my friends as Jonathan had with David. He served him
so well, doing whatever David's soul desired. That is servant
love, the kind You continually show us. Help me to be a better
friend. Let me know what to say, when to speak, and whom to
encourage. I want to do Your will in the world. Lead me on!

My Stresses

The Power of Rest and Refreshment

Come to Me, all you who labor and are heavy-laden and overburdened, and I will cause you to rest. [I will ease and relieve and refresh your souls.]
MATTHEW 11:28 AMP

*S*ome days we are pulled and pushed and stretched every which way. As the pressures of living mount, we feel our sense of well-being slowly disintegrating. At times even our home may be a source of tension in the form of strained relationships between family members. During such adversity our true colors tend to show, revealing who we are and where we are putting our trust.

Tim Elmore writes, "If we place our faith in the doctor to heal us, or our jobs to pay us, or our supervisors to provide our sense of identity—our faith has been misplaced, and pressure will reveal this one day. Those instruments will fail to provide all we need. Our faith must be firmly placed in God, the great Provider. Anything else, and pressure will reveal our weakness."[39]

Stress is not a new problem. Remember Elijah? After an amazing victory on Mount Carmel, we find this prophet running for his life as fear replaced faith. First Kings 19 tells us that once he made his escape, Elijah rested beneath a broom tree where he "prayed that he might die. 'I have had enough, LORD,' he said. 'Take my life'" (verse 4 NIV). Then he lay down and fell asleep.

Have you ever felt like Elijah, saying, "Lord, I can't take it anymore," and then fallen into bed? But fortunately, as He did to Elijah, God is ready to minister to us in the midst of stress, to feed us and give us rest on every side, to fuel us with direction, compassion, and encouragement.

Stress is nothing new. Since Adam and Eve, people have always been under some sort of pressure—but it's important to understand that stress today is linked to such health problems as cancer, heart disease, accidental injuries, suicide, and depression. "In recent years," writes Gordon MacDonald, "it has become very clear that many people in our society are under constant and destructive stress as life for them operates at a pace that offers little time for any restorative rest and retreat."[40]

Ah, rest and retreat. . .but where to find a broom tree? Perhaps it would be easier for us to find a broom *closet*, a quiet, personal place of prayer (see Matthew 6:6 KJV), and there seek out the One on whom we have built our house—Jesus Christ (see Matthew 7:24–27). He alone is the One who can get us through the storms of this life. Now that we know where to go and who to turn to, what can we do to protect ourselves against stress, to shore up our foundation of trust in God, so that our true color will be a consistent and overwhelming peace of Christ—within and without?

The first protective measure against stress is to make sure we take a weekly Sabbath rest. Spend time in His presence, reading God's Word and Christian literature. Feed your mind as you rest your body. In your quiet time, give the Spirit a chance to light upon you, giving you discernment, realigning your priorities, and allowing you to see your life, circumstances, needs, and desires through the eyes of God.

Second, take a *daily* Sabbath rest, something our Lord did on a regular basis. Luke 5:16 says, "Jesus often withdrew to lonely places and prayed" (NIV). When you eagerly seek the Lord throughout the day, you will find Him and He will give you rest on every side (see 2 Chronicles 15:15).

Third, focus on and trust in God. In times of anxiety, we tend to let fear replace faith. We feel like Job: "What I feared has come upon me; what I dreaded has happened to me. I have no peace, no quietness; I have no rest, but only turmoil" (Job 3:25–26 NIV). Constantly remind yourself that with Jesus, you have nothing to fear. You can trust in the One who will never leave you nor forsake you. Continually shore up that trust by claiming God's promises, reading the Word, and applying it to your life. Keep your eye on Christ, not your fears or circumstances.

Fourth, daily ask God to help you keep your peace and give you joy on the journey through life, knowing that stress, although tortuous at times, *can* make you a stronger person (see James 1:2–4). All the while keep in mind that no matter how difficult a situation may seem, nothing is impossible with God.

Finally, give your burdens to Jesus and leave them there. His shoulders were made to carry them. " 'Come to Me, all you who labor and are heavy laden, and I will give you rest' " (Matthew 11:28 NKJV).

Continually turn to God, resting in His presence, trusting in Him, and allowing Him to carry your load. Build your life not on the world and its pleasures but on His words, hearing them and putting them into practice (see Matthew 7:24), and your foundation will be structurally sound, able to resist the cracks brought on by the storms of life.

Christ beneath me.

On Eagles' Wings

"I carried you on eagles' wings and brought you to myself."
EXODUS 19:4 NIV

*G*od, I need You to lift me up, above all these problems, above my circumstances, above my helplessness. Carry me off to Your place in the heavenlies, where I can find my breath, where I can sit with You, where I can find the peace of Your presence. You alone can carry me through this. I feel myself drifting off, Your strong arms holding me close, Your breath touching my face. Thank You, Lord, for saving my soul. My spirit rejoices!

Emergency Call

A hostile world! I called to GOD, to my God I cried out. From his palace he heard me call; my cry brought me right into his presence — a private audience!
2 SAMUEL 22:7 THE MESSAGE

*T*his trial, this thing I'm going through, Lord, I don't know how to handle it. I don't know what to do. But I am certain of one thing and one thing only: You can handle it. You hear me when I cry out to You and You bring me directly into Your presence. You are ready to listen to me, to my groanings and my pleas. Help me, Lord, to find the strength to carry on.

Needing Direction

Thus says the LORD: "Stand in the ways and see, and ask for the old paths, where the good way is, and walk in it; then you will find rest for your souls."
JEREMIAH 6:16 NKJV

*L*ord, I come before You, standing here, seeking Your face. I need direction. I feel so lost, so alone. But You are here with me, to lead and to guide me, to show me the way I should go. With You and You alone, I can find rest for my soul. Give me the peace of Jesus. Peace like a river. Peace. . . Peace. . . Peace. . . Lord, give me peace.

Running to God

As the deer pants for the water brooks, so my soul pants for You, O God. My soul thirsts for God, for the living God.
PSALM 42:1–2 NASB

I have been running, running, running in all different directions, but I need to run to You now and stay here in Your presence. I am thirsting for You as I have never thirsted before. My future looks bleak. I cannot see beyond my troubles. But I now focus on Your light. It warms my skin, touches my heart, and speaks to my soul. I join my spirit with Yours and rest here at Your feet.

Pile It on Jesus

Pile your troubles on GOD's shoulders — he'll carry your load, he'll help you out.
He'll never let good people topple into ruin. . . . I trust in [God].
PSALM 55:22–23 THE MESSAGE

*L*ord, my burdens are so heavy. My bones hurt from all the pressure. With each breath I take, I draw myself closer to You. With each beat of my heart, I am nearer to Your peace. Touch my body, Lord, and my heart and soul. My spirit wants to cling to You for strength, love, and compassion. Take away the hurt and fill me with Your strength. Help me to relax in Your presence. Give me a good word from Your lips. Take the burdens from me. Help me to leave them at Your feet.

Lifted out of the Pit

"Do not fear, for I am with you; do not anxiously look about you, for I am your God.
I will strengthen you, surely I will help you,
surely I will uphold you with My righteous right hand.'"
ISAIAH 41:10 NASB

I am in such turmoil. I don't understand what's happening or why. All I know is that I am stressed out and I can't seem to get a handle on anything anymore. Lift me up out of this pit, Lord. I trust in You. I know that You can uphold me, that You can help me rise above my troubles, for You have overcome this world. I know that I am precious in Your sight and You will not allow evil to harm me. Save me, lift me, meet me now!

True Colors

Consider it a sheer gift, friends, when tests and challenges come at you from all sides. You know that under pressure, your faith-life is forced into the open and shows its true colors. So don't try to get out of anything prematurely. Let it do its work so you become mature and well-developed, not deficient in any way.

JAMES 1:2–4 THE MESSAGE

*L*ord, I haven't been handling the stress very well lately. How do I let myself get into these situations? I know I am to consider it a challenge when I am under pressure, but right now I feel like I'm challenged out. Help me to find joy in the journey, Lord. To remember that no matter what happens, You are on this ride with me. May the pressure that is on me now make me more like Christ. Lord, I pray for Your peace!

Days of Trouble

In the day of my trouble I will call on You, for You will answer me.

PSALM 86:7 AMP

*E*verywhere I go, everywhere I look—at home, the office, the world—things are falling apart. There's trouble right here. And I don't know what to do. At times I feel as if this world is careening out of control. Between terrorist threats, the economy, and the war, there seems to be no peace. But yet when I come to You, I can have peace. Your peace. Speak to me, Lord. Answer me when I call. Help my spirit to rest in You, in this moment and throughout this day.

Beaten Down

We've been surrounded and battered by troubles, but we're not demoralized;
we're not sure what to do, but we know that God knows what to do;
we've been spiritually terrorized, but God hasn't left our side;
we've been thrown down, but we haven't broken.

2 Corinthians 4:8–9 the message

I think this is the worst day of my life, Lord. I am totally beaten down. I have been pushed around, strung up, held down, kicked out. The influence of the evil one seems to be surrounding me. I can hardly catch my breath. I feel like Elijah. I have had enough, Lord! Help me! The only thing getting me through this is coming into Your presence, remembering that You are by my side through it all. Thank You, Lord, for going through this with me. Help me to focus on You and not on my circumstances. Help me to live in You.

Blessings amid the Storm

I said to myself, "Relax and rest. God has showered you with blessings."

Psalm 116:7 the message

*L*ord, when I look back on all the ways You have blessed me and continue to bless me, even through these trials, I am awed and thankful. As You have delivered me in the past, deliver me again from the troubles before me. Lift the burdens off my sagging shoulders. I leave them at the foot of Your cross, as instructed. Thank You, Lord. I love You so much. Now with each breath I take, I relax and enter into Your rest.

Sabbath Rest

They rested quietly on the Sabbath, as commanded.
LUKE 23:56 THE MESSAGE

*A*nother Sunday! Another day I get to spend more time with You. It doesn't get any better than this. I have made a commitment, Lord, to spend all day with You, worshiping with my church family, reading Your Word, resting in Your presence. It would be great if every day were like this. Help me to keep the peace I feel today throughout the week ahead. I want to live my life in Sabbath rest. I want to seek You every moment of every day.

Flying Away to Safety

My heart is grievously pained within me. . . . Fear and trembling have come upon me; horror and fright have overwhelmed me. And I say, Oh, that I had wings like a dove! I would fly away and be at rest. . . . I will call upon God, and the Lord will save me.
PSALM 55:4, 5–6, 16 AMP

*M*y heart is so heavy it hurts. Lift the burden from me, Lord. Take away these feelings of fear. All I want to do is run away, fly out of here. I lift my soul unto You, Lord, seeking Your face, Your peace, Your rest. I call out to You, Lord. "Save me! Lift me! Take me into Your presence!" With each cry of my heart and tear from my eye, I come closer to You, where I am safe, where nothing can harm me, where I can be at peace.

My Comfort

GOD, my shepherd! I don't need a thing. You have bedded me down in lush meadows,
you find me quiet pools to drink from. True to your word, you let me
catch my breath and send me in the right direction.
PSALM 23:1–3 THE MESSAGE

*A*h, here I come, ready to leap into Your arms. I need to feel Your presence surrounding me. I know You, my Good Shepherd, will take care of me. You will take me to a place where I can rest. You will lead me to a place where the water is still. You are an oasis in this hectic world, a world I am leaving behind right now. For now I am with You. You will send me in the right direction. You will lead me closer to You. Protect me, love me, guide me, touch me. Breathe on me, breath of God.

The Secret Joy in Jesus

He who dwells in the secret place of the Most High shall remain stable and fixed under
the shadow of the Almighty [Whose power no foe can withstand].
PSALM 91:1 AMP

I come to You today, meeting You in that secret place where I know I am safe. You are my Rock, my Sure Foundation. Hiding in You, I will come to no harm. I rest in this place, seeking Your face. Jesus, Jesus, Jesus. There is magic in that name. There is peace in this place. There is love in Your eyes. I praise Your holy name! I smile in Your presence. You are the joy of my life!

My Church

The Power of Unity

Now the multitude of those who believed were of one heart and one soul. . . . And with great power the apostles gave witness to the resurrection of the Lord Jesus. And great grace was upon them all.

ACTS 4:32–33 NKJV

*T*he ultimate power of prayer is found in a church where people of one mind unite. In the Old Testament, God decreed that "mine house shall be called an house of prayer for all people" (Isaiah 56:7 KJV), and in the New Testament Jesus tells us that "where two or three are gathered together in my name, there am I in the midst of them" (Matthew 18:20 KJV). God's decree, Jesus' promised presence, and our unity of mind combine to create one of the most powerful forces on earth—a united, praying church!

The need to come together in prayer and worship is an integral part of our makeup. In Genesis we read, "the LORD God said, It is not good that the man should be alone" (2:18 KJV). We were *created* to come together before God.

When Jesus taught us how to pray, He didn't begin with "*My* Father which art in heaven" but "*Our* Father which art in heaven." He continued: "Give *us* this day *our* daily bread. And forgive *us our* debts, as *we* forgive *our* debtors. And lead *us* not into temptation, but deliver *us* from evil" (Matthew 6:9, 11–12 KJV, emphasis added). Through this one lesson, could the Son of God have made it any clearer that prayer was to be a corporate effort of united minds?

The church, as a force of unity, was first seen in the book of Acts. After Jesus' death, His disciples gathered in the upper room "with *one accord* in prayer and supplication" (1:14 KJV, emphasis added) to await the promised Holy Spirit. And on the day of Pentecost when they were again "all with *one accord* in one place" (2:1 KJV, emphasis added), they heard the rush of a mighty wind that filled the house where they were. Here God met them and blessed them, pouring out His Spirit from on high. Afterward they had joyful fellowship, as "they, continuing daily with *one accord* in the temple, and breaking bread from house to house, did eat their meat with gladness and *singleness of heart*" (2:46 KJV, emphasis added). Later, when they "lifted up *their* voice to God with *one accord*" (4:24 KJV, emphasis added), praising Him and praying to Him, "the place was shaken where they were *assembled together*; and they were all filled with the Holy Ghost, and they spake the word of God with boldness" (4:31 KJV, emphasis added). The day on which the apostles performed an amazing amount of miracles, bringing many believers to the Lord, they were gathered with *one accord* at the temple (see 5:12 KJV).

The evidence of the power of unity, of gathering together and praying in one accord, is staggering! And it's not only the *power* felt amid Christ's presence, but the *joy*—the gladness and singleness of heart—of a holy fellowship! But the joy will be short-lived if, in service to the body, only a few souls are taking on the entire load. Such church members must beware of burnout. Larry Burkett writes, "Don't get so busy serving God that you don't have any time for Him."[41] Members suffering from burnout weaken the entire church because when one member of the body suffers, we all suffer because "we are members one of another" (Ephesians 4:25 KJV). As God's children, everyone must do his or her part.

Along with providing us a place to meet our needs and

fulfill God's desires, church provides an avenue wherein we can express our commitment to God and the body of Christ. As we express our dedication to God through our attendance in fellowship with other believers, we are moved out of self-centered isolation and reminded of the "big picture."

None of this is to say that we are not to spend time alone in prayer. In addition to corporate prayer and fellowship, we need daily to cultivate a one-on-one relationship with Jesus, immersing ourselves in His Word and learning to recognize His voice. For if we cannot distinguish His voice individually, how will we discern it corporately? Jesus said, "My sheep hear my voice, and I know them, and they follow me" (John 10:27 KJV). Training ourselves to listen and recognize our Good Shepherd's voice, both corporately and individually, is essential to our spiritual growth.

The church is where the Word of God is taught, spiritual direction gleaned, corporate prayers delivered, spiritual gifts discerned, missionaries chosen, concerns shared, encouragement given, pastors selected, and ministries performed. The body of Christ is a living body that serves a living God. And it is a place of power only when we are united in one accord, seeking and moving together in *His* will.

The church is the place where we are all reminded of the power of unity under God. It is where our focus is to be solely on the heavens above, a place where we gather with one common purpose—to love God and each other. In such a spiritual haven, in the midst of Christ's presence, fellow believers are pulled away from earthly concerns and look to Christ seated in the heavenlies with God. There is no greater joy!

Christ above me.

Edifying Others

Let us consider how to stimulate one another to love and good deeds, not forsaking our own assembling together, as is the habit of some, but encouraging one another.
HEBREWS 10:24–25 NASB

*L*ord, I will be meeting with others at church today. I want to be an encourager of Your servants, stimulating others, drawing them closer to You. Plant a good word in my heart, one I can use to edify others. Point out a verse from my Bible reading today that someone else needs to hear. Give me the right moment, the right words. And if it's a listening ear someone needs, give me the wisdom of silence. Lead me to do Your will this day.

Unceasing Prayer

Prayer was made without ceasing of the church unto God for him.
ACTS 12:5 KJV

*G*od, I remember how Peter's friends prayed for him while he was in prison, how they constantly and consistently interceded for him. You sent an angel to visit Peter and his chains fell off! Help me to be such a prayer warrior today. Lord, tell me whom to pray for this morning. And may such deliverance come to that person according to Your will.

Jesus in Our Midst

For where two or three are gathered together in my name,
there am I in the midst of them.
MATTHEW 18:20 KJV

*L*ord, it's so amazing that when we come together with other believers—even when just two believers are together—You show up! You are in the midst of us! You love us that much. Be with Your body of believers today, Lord, whenever and wherever they are meeting around the world. Show them Your power, Your presence. Answer their prayers today, Lord. All to Your glory!

Testimony of Believers

They were heartily welcomed by the church and the apostles and the elders,
and they told them all that God had accomplished through them.
ACTS 15:4 AMP

*L*ord, when I hear what other people say You have done in their lives, their testimonies buoy my own faith. It gives me chills when I hear of the wonders of Your deeds. Give me the courage to share my testimony with others, knowing this will draw unbelievers to You and strengthen the hearts of those who already know You. Thank You, Lord, for hearing my prayer.

Missions

Then it seemed good to the apostles and the elders, with the whole church,
to choose men from among them and send them to Antioch.
ACTS 15:22 ESV

I don't know if I could serve in a foreign country, Lord, but there are others who will and do. God bless them. Give them strength and protection in these perilous days. Speak to their hearts. Specifically I pray for [your church's missionaries' names]. Make their message clear. Aid them in their journey. Open the hearts of those around them who dwell in darkness. Spread Your light among the nations, O God.

Ministers

If you have the gift of speaking, preach God's message. If you have the gift
of helping others, do it with the strength that God supplies. Everything should
be done in a way that will bring honor to God because of Jesus Christ,
who is glorious and powerful forever. Amen.
1 PETER 4:11 CEV

I bring before You this morning the minister of my church. Give him strength as he comforts, counsels, and consoles the sheep of his flock. Help him as he prepares the sermon for this Sunday, meets with the church leaders, and goes throughout his week. Protect him from the evil that surrounds him. Fill him with Your light, anoint him with Your Spirit, and give him the Word his people need to hear.

One Body

We are members one of another.
EPHESIANS 4:25 KJV

*W*hen one of us is suffering, Lord, we all hurt. Some of my church are grieving, some are burned out, some are of ill health and unsound mind, and some are in financial distress. Lord, bless the people who make up the body of my church. Give them love and comfort. Make this body a unified body, strengthened by Your Spirit and Your love, gathered to meet in Your presence, formed to do Your will.

Singing Praise

Saying, I will declare thy name unto my brethren,
in the midst of the church will I sing praise unto thee.
HEBREWS 2:12 KJV

*A*ll I want to do in church is sing, Lord. I don't care what kind of music it is—contemporary or traditional—as long as it edifies You. All I know is that I want to be with fellow believers and in Your presence. Give me amazing grace to stand with my fellow believers in the midst of the church and sing praises unto You. Thank You for the joy of music, Lord!

Church Division

When you come together as a church, I hear that divisions exist among you.
1 CORINTHIANS 11:18 NASB

*L*ord, how can those who are united in belief be so divided in other areas? Please, God, You know what is causing strife in Your house of prayer. Please soothe it with Your healing balm. Give our leaders and members wisdom. Pour out upon us Your love and remind us of the love we have for each other. Heal the breach, Lord. I put all these concerns in Your hands. Give me the wisdom to leave them there.

Servants of the Church

Now you are the body of Christ, and members individually. And God has appointed these in the church: first apostles, second prophets, third teachers, after that miracles, then gifts of healings, helps, administrations, varieties of tongues.
1 CORINTHIANS 12:27–28 NKJV

*I*t's amazing how many talents people have. Please, Lord, bless those who are gifted and who are helping to serve Your body. Give them wisdom, energy, and time to do what You have designed. Help them not to get burned out. And for those who are just sitting in the pew, please speak to their hearts, urging them to set their hands to a task for You. Thank You for the gifts You have given to me. Help me to use them for Your glory.

Edify the Church

Since you are eager to have spiritual gifts,
try to excel in gifts that build up the church.
1 CORINTHIANS 14:12 NIV

*L*ord, I'm eager to serve You, but I'm not really sure what my gift is. And I don't want to make a fool of myself by trying something and having it be a flop. Give me guidance as to where, when, and how You want me to serve. Give me a gift that will build up Your church. Speak to me clearly as I go throughout this day and the days to come. And if there ever does come a time when You want me to bow out of a ministry, give me the wisdom to do so.

Foundation of Truth

The church of the living God is the strong foundation of truth.
1 TIMOTHY 3:15 CEV

*T*here is no stronger foundation than that of Your truth, which is what our church is built upon. We are not a church made up of stone, stucco, brick, or wood but of people from all walks of life. We are a church of the Living God. Oh, what a glorious thing! Make our church strong, Lord, so that we can shine Your light into our community, state, and world!

Sunday Morning Prayer

With one mind and one mouth glorify the God and Father of our Lord Jesus Christ.
ROMANS 15:6 NKJV

*U*nite our minds and mouths, Lord, and lift them up to Your glory and the glory of Your Son Jesus. We want to feel the power of unity as we come before You in all our ministries and worship. There is nothing like united believers coming together to seek You, all of one accord. Like the disciples at Pentecost, we want to feel the power of Your mighty wind as we gather together in Your house of prayer. Unite us, Lord, to Your glory, forever and ever!

Fellowship

That which we have seen and heard we proclaim also to you, so that you too may have fellowship with us; and indeed our fellowship is with the Father and with his Son Jesus Christ.
1 JOHN 1:3 ESV

*W*hen we gather together in Your house, we not only have fellowship with each other, but we meet with You, Your Son, and Your Spirit. Breathe on us, Lord. Allow us to unite in prayer and feel Your presence among us. Lead us to the font of eternal blessing and give us strength to do Your will and wisdom to apply Your Word. Increase our body as You did with the early church in the beginning of the book of Acts. We want to see new believers come to experience Your peace and Your love!

My Work

The Power of Commitment

Commit your work to the LORD, and your plans will be established.
PROVERBS 16:4 NRSV

*K*nowing He was soon to be sacrificed for our sins, Jesus prayed to God, " 'I have glorified You on the earth. I have finished the work You have given Me to do' " (John 17:4 NKJV).

God the Potter has created each of us for a specific purpose and continually shapes us as it seems good to Him (see Jeremiah 18:4). For what has God fashioned you? If you're not sure, pray for guidance, with a mind open enough to accept whatever the Lord tells you. Romans 12:2 says, "Let God. . .give you a new mind. Then you will know what God wants you to do" (NLV). Such seeking is an ongoing process. God's direction must persistently be petitioned since today's work may merely be the training ground for the job He has planned but we have yet to discover.

Once you have prayed and heard God's direction, have the courage to walk where He leads, remembering that He will always go before you (see Isaiah 52:12). Don't let fear give you lead feet. Instead, rest in the assurance that God will "give you every good thing you need so you can do what He wants" (Hebrews 13:21 NLV). God will give you courage, gifts, and opportunities, as well as combine your experience, talents, and knowledge, in order to place you where He needs you. Each day tap into the power of commitment, keeping your course steady so that you will be amply rewarded, now and at the end of your journey, as a "good and faithful servant" (Matthew 25:23 NLV).

As you perform your work, you need to remember that you are an ambassador of Christ. Larry Burkett writes, "Our true Christian beliefs will be reflected in our work situation, as we interface with others, more than in any other environment outside the immediate family relationships."[42]

To help you interact with coworkers in a Christlike way, pray for the power to live not by worldly standards but by God's Word. This exercise will enable you to avoid four worldly traps, the first being the tendency to compare your job, pay, or duties with those of others. "Everyone should look at himself and see how he does his own work. Then he can be happy in what he has done. He should not compare himself with his neighbor" (Galatians 6:4 NLV). Thank God for your present job, perform the tasks He has given you, and work to His honor. As the expression goes, bloom where you are planted, working with all your heart, because you are working "for the Lord and not for men" (Colossians 3:23 NLV).

Second, don't let the daily grind of routine crush your spirit. "There is nothing better for a man than to. . .find joy in his work. I have seen that this also is from the hand of God. For who can. . .find joy without Him? (Ecclesiastes 2:24–25 NLV). So whether your job is performing repetitive household chores, running the widget-making machine, or teaching the same old lesson plan year after year, find joy in the journey. Don't let the monotony of life get you down, but keep *God* first in your life, "for the kingdom of God is. . .righteousness, peace and joy in the Holy Spirit" (Romans 14:17 NIV).

Third, don't become so immersed in your present job that you miss the opportunities God puts in your path. Because God gives you both the means and the desire to fulfill your purpose for Him, He may prompt you to take some evening courses, invest in a hobby, or change jobs. All of these stepping-stones may be training for future endeavors. If you're too involved in your current job, you may miss His promptings. Workaholics neglect their family, church, friends, and God. Don't go to heaven wishing you'd spent more time with the wife and kids rather than at the office. Keep your work in balance with the rest of your life.

Finally, don't work just for the money. Frederick Buechner writes, "If [a man's] in it only for the money, the money is all he gains, and when he finally retires, he may well ask himself if it was worth giving most of his life for."[43] We must beware of having our eyes on the wrong treasure to the detriment of our souls. Jesus said, "You say that you are rich and need nothing, but you do not know that you are so troubled in mind and heart" (Revelation 3:17 NLV). Put your heart and soul into whatever you set your hand to, doing it to serve others and God, not mammon.

Daily commit your work to God and consistently seek His direction. Remember that He continually opens doors for His children (see 1 Corinthians 16:9; 2 Corinthians 2:12; and Colossians 4:3)—but keep your ears open to His voice and your eyes open to opportunity. Through all your life's work, consistently ask Christ for His advice and direction, remembering that all "works committed to God will be supported by God."[44]

Christ on my right.

Guided by the Holy Spirit

Let the Holy Spirit lead you in each step. . . . If the Holy Spirit is living in us,
let us be led by Him in all things.
GALATIANS 5:16, 25 NLV

I understand, Lord, that the Holy Spirit is just waiting to lead me. Open my mind and heart and ears to His voice today. Still the constant chatter in my head that keeps reminding me of all the tasks I need to get done today. Give me the plan You have already laid out for my life. Shape me into the person You want me to be so that I can do what You have created me to do. Lead me step by step, Lord. I commit my way and my plans to Your purpose.

My Purpose

The LORD has made everything for its purpose.
PROVERBS 16:4 NRSV

*L*ord, what am I supposed to do? I'm not sure why I'm at this job. Or am I not to have a career but be a stay-at-home parent? Have I made the wrong decision? Am I walking in Your will, or have I been led by my own desires? Show me, Lord, which way You want me to go. If there is some new challenge You want me to undertake, please tell me. Let me hear Your voice. Renew my mind this morning so that I can know Your good and perfect will for my life.

Spirit-Filled

"I have filled him with the Spirit of God in wisdom, understanding,
much learning, and all kinds of special work."
EXODUS 31:3 NLV

*Y*ou have filled me with Your Spirit. I have been given wisdom, understanding, education, and talent for many lines of work. Show me how I can use my knowledge, understanding, and abilities to do the work You have set out for me. Show me the paths You want me to take. What do You want me to do with my hands, my life, my gifts? They are all from You, the One I want to serve.

A New Mind

Let God change your life. First of all, let Him give you a new mind. Then you will know
what God wants you to do. And the things you do will be good and pleasing and perfect.
ROMANS 12:2 NLV

I'm so confused, Lord. I seem to have the wrong mindset today. Instead of looking to Your leading, I seem to be focused in on the worldly aspects of life. And I know that's not where You want my thoughts to be. Give me the mind of Christ. Make my needs simple. Change my life, my thoughts, my desires. I want to live a life that is good, perfect, and pleasing to You.

The Right God

"If you ever forget the Lord your God and go to other gods to worship and work for them,
I tell you today that you will be destroyed for sure."

DEUTERONOMY 8:19 NLV

*L*ord, I don't want to live my life working for money, power, possessions, position, or status. I want to live for You, work for You, be with You. Keep Yourself in the forefront of my mind this morning and throughout this day. You are the One I worship and the One I serve. You and no one else. Live through me this day. Give me joy in the journey. Lead me to the font of eternal blessing. Thank You, Lord, for saving my soul for Your use!

God Gives the Power

"Be careful not to say in your heart, 'My power and strong hand have made me rich.'
But remember the Lord your God. For it is He Who is giving you power to become rich."

DEUTERONOMY 8:17–18 NLV

*Y*ou are the One who has brought me to where I am today. Thank You, God, for giving me power and strength. All the blessings I have in this life come from Your hand. Continue to lead me in Your way. My ears desperately seek to hear Your voice. My heart longs for Your presence. Although I may not be rich in a worldly sense, I am rich in my love of You. Further my knowledge and increase my talents so that I can do the work You desire.

A Place for My Gifts

Be sure to use the gift God gave you.
1 TIMOTHY 4:14 NLV

*L*ord, I'm not currently using the gifts I believe You gave me. Help me find a place where I can use my talents, experience, and knowledge to Your good. And while I am in my current position, help me to do my work for Your glory, because You are the manager of my life. Give me Your peace, joy, and direction. I so desperately need to spend these moments in Your presence to prepare my spirit for the tasks of this day. Do not leave me, Lord. Stay in my heart now and forever.

Working to His Honor

Do everything to honor God.
1 CORINTHIANS 10:31 NLV

*E*verything I do and everything I have is for Your honor and Your glory—not mine! I am the ambassador of Your one and only Son, Jesus Christ. Give me that attitude today, so that everyone who looks at me, hears me, and speaks to me will see His face and feel His presence. I want to become less so that He can become more. I am Your servant, Lord—help me to serve productively and creatively. All, Lord, to Your honor!

Things Needful and Good

May God give you every good thing you need so you can do what He wants. . . . May
Christ have all the shining-greatness forever! Let it be so.
HEBREWS 13:21 NLV

*L*ord, I want to do what You want me to do. In order to accomplish that, there are a few things I need—Your gifting, direction, strength, and power. Fill me with these things as I commit my life, my work, my day to You. And at the end of the day and the end of my life, may You say to me, "Well done, good and faithful servant!" And may Christ have all the glory. Lord, let it be so!

The Comparison Trap

Everyone should look at himself and see how he does his own work. Then he can be
happy in what he has done. He should not compare himself with his neighbor.
GALATIANS 6:4 NLV

*L*ord, I keep comparing myself and my work to others, and I know that's not what You want me to do. Help me to keep my eyes on You and Your direction for my life, not on what I have or don't have. I want to be happy in this life and in what I have accomplished. Don't let me fall into the comparison trap. Thank You for the job I have now, for the pay I receive, and for the ability to serve others the best way I know how.

The Right Attitude

Be glad you can do the things you should be doing. Do all things without arguing and talking about how you wish you did not have to do them.

PHILIPPIANS 2:14 NLV

I'm getting tired of my job and my boss, Lord. It seems like the same thing day in and day out. I know I should be grateful for the work I have been given, but I can't seem to get past this wall of negativity. Give me the right mindset, Lord, before I even go into work. And then help me remember that I am working for You. Give me the mind and servant attitude of Christ this morning and help me maintain it throughout this day.

Joyful Servant

" 'You have done well. You are a good and faithful servant. You have been faithful over a few things. I will put many things in your care. Come and share my joy.' "

MATTHEW 25:23 NLV

I want to be a good and faithful servant sharing Your joy, but I feel like the world is bringing me down. That and my job. Help me to be faithful in what You have given me and then, if it is Your will, put more things in my care. I want to feel and share the joy that working for and with You brings. Help me to renew my mind this morning, because my head is definitely in the wrong place. Touch me with Your compassion and grace. Fill me with Your Spirit, Your joy, Your love.

Great Expectations

"David. . .served his own generation by the will of God."
ACTS 13:36 KJV

*L*ord, I want to be like David, serving my own generation by Your will. No matter how small the job or role, fill me with great expectations, that You are going to do a powerful work through me. I ask this not for my glory, but to demonstrate to others the power of living in You. Imbue me with hope and thanksgiving. I do not know the entire plan You have for my life. Help me not to look too far ahead and thus miss the joy of day-to-day living. Thank You for hearing this prayer.

His Work Plan

We will follow the plan of the work He has given us to do.
2 CORINTHIANS 10:13 NLV

*M*y goal is to live the life You have planned for me. Keep me on the road to Your will. Show me the ways You want me to go. Help me avoid the worldly traps of money, discontentment, grief, envy, workaholism, and tedium. Keep me close to Your side and consistently in Your presence, ever open to hearing Your voice. Give me the power to live Your plan for me. Thank You for all You are doing in my life!

My Relationships

The Power of Forgiveness

"And when you stand praying, if you hold anything against anyone, forgive him, so that your Father in heaven may forgive you your sins."

MARK 11:25 NIV

*R*elationships—between you and God, you and yourself, and you and others—can be a fragile thing. And when such relationships are breached, you can be sure the bane of unforgiveness is at the core.

When I think of the power of forgiveness, I am reminded of my friends and fellow church members, the late Eva and Roland Detweiler. Years ago, their son had been murdered, stabbed to death in his apartment. Although the Detweilers had been devastated at their loss, this godly couple attended the killer's trial and, in fact, met and prayed with him. They forgave the one who had taken their beloved son's life. When I first heard their story, during a Sunday school class on the topic of forgiveness, I was stunned. I wondered how they could have forgiven their son's murderer, how they had managed to get on with their lives without bitterness, how they could continue to be such peaceful people. The answer was simple: Their wounds and spirits had been healed by the power of forgiveness, a gift from God.

Forgiving those who offend us is difficult at best. The more heinous the infraction, the harder it is to pardon the perpetrator.

Yet that is exactly what Jesus calls us to do. Granted, forgiving someone who murders your child is much harder than forgiving the individual who speaks ill of you. But words can be as sharp as the blade of a killer's knife. It amazes me how family squabbles can keep siblings and other family members from talking to each other for the rest of their lives—or how one careless word from a friend can sever a lifelong relationship.

It has been said that refusing to forgive someone who injures you is like drinking poison and expecting the offender to die. David Jeremiah writes, "The only way to heal the pain that will not heal itself is to forgive the person who hurt you. Forgiving heals your memory as you change your memory's vision. When you release the wrongdoer from your wrath, you cut a malignant tumor out of your own life. You set a prisoner free. . .and discover that the prisoner you freed was yourself."[45]

But if we know there is such freedom in forgiveness, why does it seem so hard? We must ask ourselves, "If Jesus can be stripped naked, beaten, scourged, have nails driven into his hands and feet, hang on a cross until death, and still say, 'Father, forgive them for they know what not they do' (see Luke 23:34), why can't we?" "Oh well," you say, "it was easy for Him. He was God." Yet God insists we forgive others no matter how big or small the offenses. But how do we tap into His power of forgiveness?

The first step is to allow yourself to feel the hurt of the offenses against you, both past and present. Pray for the release of that hurt, and then pray for the power to forgive as God constantly and consistently forgives you. Continue to pray until you have truly forgiven in your heart. (It may not happen immediately, but it *will* happen.) Then thank God for His goodness and peace. Finally, when the time is right, try to restore your relationship with the person who hurt you. Pray for the right words to say. Someone has to be willing to take the first step—and that someone is you. All the while, keep in mind that, although your offender's behavior may not change, you will, becoming more like Christ!

Sometimes the one you need to forgive is yourself. Remember how Peter claimed he would never deny Christ and then turned around and did just that not once but *three* times? Oswald Chambers writes, "After Peter's denial the isolation of misery would inevitably have seized on him and made him want to retire in the mood of 'I can never forgive myself,' had not our Lord forestalled this by giving him something positive to do—'When you have returned to Me, strengthen your brethren' (Luke 22:32 NKJV)."[46]

If you have offended yourself or God, talk to Him. Ask for His forgiveness, and then try to do better the next time. Don't constantly berate yourself for your bad behavior, toward either yourself or others. God does not forgive us based on how well we perform or how acceptable we believe we are in His sight. He forgives us based on the sacrifice of Jesus Christ. Oswald Chambers writes, "Forgiveness means not merely that I am saved from sin and made right for heaven. . . . Forgiveness means that I am forgiven into a recreated relationship, into identification with God in Christ."[47]

Don't poison yourself with the bitter pill of *unforgiveness*—it's suicide! Instead, tap into the power of *forgiveness*, keeping Jesus' peace in mind, His mercy in your heart, His power at hand, and your relationships whole.

Christ on my left.

Two-Way Forgiveness

"And when you stand praying, if you hold anything against anyone, forgive him, so that your Father in heaven may forgive you your sins."
MARK 11:25 NIV

*I*t's a two-way street, Lord—we forgive others and then You will forgive us. I know I've read that scripture a hundred times, but I've never understood it more fully than today. Give me the strength of Your forgiveness this morning, Lord. Help me to love and not hate the person who has hurt me. Thank You for releasing the poison of unforgiveness that has been building up within me.

God Knows My Coworker's Heart

"Then hear from heaven Your dwelling place, and forgive, and render to each according to all his ways, whose heart You know for You alone know the hearts of the sons of men."
2 CHRONICLES 6:30 NASB

*L*ord, You can see into everyone's heart. You know the good and the bad in all of us. Right now, I feel as if my coworker has inflicted only his "bad" upon me. Yet perhaps other things are going on in his life that I cannot see and do not know. But You know all. Please, Lord, help me to forgive him as You forgive me. And when I see him today, give me peace in my heart, the right words to say, and lots of love.

Forgiving My Friend

"Be alert. If you see your friend going wrong, correct him. If he responds, forgive him. Even if it's personal against you and repeated seven times through the day, and seven times he says, 'I'm sorry, I won't do it again,' forgive him."

LUKE 17:3–4 THE MESSAGE

I've about had it, Lord. I don't know how much more of this I can take! Is this friendship even worth all this pain? Lord, please calm me down. Give me the right attitude. Your Word says that no matter how many times I am offended, if my friend apologizes and says she'll never do it again, I am to forgive her. Well, You're going to have to give me this power, because I have none left of my own. Please work, live, and love through me. Help me to forgive my friend.

Easily Offended

"I will give you a new heart and put a new spirit within you. I will take away your heart of stone and give you a heart of flesh."

EZEKIEL 36:26 NLV

*L*ord, I have such anger within me for all the wrongs done me all day long. Even when I'm out in traffic and someone cuts me off, I'm really miffed. Or when my family comes to the dinner table and no one appreciates how hard I've worked to make this meal but complains about every little thing, I just want to scream! Give me that new heart. Empty this heart of stone, the one so easily offended. Fill it with Your love.

No Guilt Trips, Please

Now is the time to forgive this man and help him back on his feet. If all you do is pour on the guilt, you could very well drown him in it. My counsel now is to pour on the love.
2 CORINTHIANS 2:7–8 THE MESSAGE

I don't know why, Lord, but I just keep bringing up old offenses and throwing them into the faces of those who have hurt me. I know that's not how You want me to behave. If I keep on this course, there's no telling how many people I will alienate from my life. And I'm not being a very good example of a Christian. Help me to forgive others and not remind them of past misdeeds. Help me to pour out Your love to all.

Spreading the Power of Forgiveness

[Jesus said,] "When you have returned to Me, strengthen your brethren."
LUKE 22:32 NKJV

*L*ord, when Peter denied You three times, he wept bitterly. I know just how he felt. But You *knew* that's what he was going to do, and You gave him words to keep him from wallowing in self-pity. You told Peter to strengthen his brethren after he turned back to You. So, I come before You this morning, asking You to forgive me and help me to forgive myself. Then, Lord, give me the opportunity to strengthen others who are dealing with unforgiveness. Help me encourage them to reconcile with those who they have hurt or who have hurt them. All for Your glory, Lord.

Needing Mercy

People who conceal their sins will not prosper, but if they confess and turn from them, they will receive mercy.
PROVERBS 28:13 NLT

*L*ord, I am so mad at myself. I have been doing wrong and hiding it from everyone. I even imagined I could hide it from You, but You know all. Lord, please forgive me for not admitting my sins to You. Help me to do better. I don't want to live this way. Sometimes I can't stand myself. Please help me to turn from this behavior. Give me Your never-ending mercy and eternal loving-kindness.

Forgiving My Pastor

"Then if my people who are called by my name will humble themselves and pray and seek my face and turn from their wicked ways, I will hear from heaven and will forgive their sins and restore their land."
2 CHRONICLES 7:14 NLT

*Y*ou'd think the one person you could trust would be your pastor. But when that trust is violated, there is much dissension in and harm to the church. Lord, I come to You today asking You to help my church family forgive its pastor. We're only human, Lord, and if he has come before You and asked for Your forgiveness, if he has truly repented, Lord, it is up to us to forgive him as well. And when we do, You will heal our church. So, Lord, give me that power of forgiveness. Forgive my pastor. Heal our church family.

Forgive Me!

If I say, "My foot slips," Your mercy, O LORD, will hold me up. In the multitude of my anxieties within me, Your comforts delight my soul.

PSALM 94:18–19 NKJV

*G*od, I've messed up again. I can hardly forgive myself. But when my foot slips, Your mercy holds me up! Forgive my offenses, Lord. Take away this feeling of anxiety within me. Help me to stop belittling and berating myself. My confidence is so low. Comfort my soul with Your presence, Your love, Your Spirit. And as You keep forgiving me, help me to forgive others.

Forgive and Forget

"Their sins and their lawless deeds I will remember no more."

HEBREWS 10:17 NASB

*W*hy can't I forgive and forget, Lord? Please help me forgive the person who injured me the other day. Instill in me Your power, Your grace, and Your mercy. With each breath I take in Your presence, I feel that power growing within me. Thank You, Lord. Now, please give me the means to forget this pain. I don't want to keep bringing it up and picking at the wound. Help me, Lord, as weak as I am, to forgive the offender and forget the pain.

No Room for the Evil One

When angry, do not sin; do not ever let your wrath (your exasperation, your fury or indignation) last until the sun goes down. Leave no [such] room or foothold for the devil [give no opportunity to him].
EPHESIANS 4:26–27 AMP

*W*hen I can't forgive, when I can't control my anger, I know I am giving the devil a foothold into my relationships and situations. And that is not a good thing. Help me to be a forgiving person, looking for healing and reconciliation instead of bitterness and retribution. You are my life and my light. Forgive me for my attitude last night and give me Your love and power today.

My Past Offenses

Keep up your reputation, GOD; forgive my bad life; it's been a very bad life.
PSALM 25:11 THE MESSAGE

*W*hen I look at my past, at the things I have done, I feel so unworthy of Your forgiveness, Lord. I can't even forgive myself. Please take pity upon me. Forgive me for all my past misdeeds. Give me a clean slate, beginning with this morning. Plant Your Word in my heart. Help me to forgive myself, as this guilt is eating away at my heart. You forgive our sins as far as the east is from the west. Thank You, God, for your mercy! Take my sins, forgive them, and make me whiter than snow in Your eyes.

Holding That Tongue

Smart people know how to hold their tongue; their grandeur is to forgive and forget.
PROVERBS 19:11 THE MESSAGE

*W*henever I bring up past misdeeds, I start the cycle of pain all over again. Why do I do that, Lord? Please stop me! Help me to hold my tongue, to think before I speak. Change my thoughts to those of Christ's. Remind me that You love those who have offended me just as much as You love me. Help me to put their need for forgiveness above my pride. Give me Your power to live this life and be the person You want me to be.

Quick Forgiveness

So, chosen by God for this new life of love, dress in the wardrobe God picked out for you: compassion, kindness, humility, quiet strength, discipline. Be even-tempered, content with second place, quick to forgive an offense. Forgive as quickly and completely as the Master forgave you. And regardless of what else you put on, wear love. It's your basic, all-purpose garment. Never be without it.
COLOSSIANS 3:12–14 THE MESSAGE

*Y*ou have chosen me to be Your child. Help me to live that life dressed in Your love. I need Your kindness, humility, quiet strength, discipline, and definitely Your even temper. Help me to forgive others as quickly as You forgive us. Do not let bitterness rot my soul. Thank You for the gift of forgiveness. Adorn me with Your love today and every day!

My Marriage

The Power of Love

Let us stop just saying we love each other; let us really show it by our actions.
1 JOHN 3:18 NLT

*I*n Preston Sturges's movie *The Palm Beach Story*, Claudette Colbert plays a wife who is bent on leaving her husband (Joel McCrea) because she thinks he could get along better and more cheaply without her. As their dispute spills out onto a New York City sidewalk, the husband desperately tries to wrestle his wife's suitcase out of her hands. When a grumpy Irish cop enters the fray, he soon finds himself prompted to give the young couple some advice: "Why don't you two try to get along together? *I* had tuh."[48]

Isn't that ultimately what marriage is all about—getting along together day in and day out? C. S. Lewis writes, "The most precious gift that marriage gave me was this constant impact of something very close and intimate yet all the time unmistakably other, resistant—in a word, real."[49]

Yes, husbands and wives are very, very real. Your spouse is the person who sleeps beside you every night, the one who is there when you wake up in the morning and when you come home. Usually that's a good thing, but there are some days that you may look over at the other side of the bed and wonder, *What was I thinking?*

Larry Burkett writes, "There are times in every marriage

when it seems barely tolerable."[50] So, after two people have fallen in love and say, "I do," how do they keep from later saying, "I don't anymore"?

First we need to understand that, from the very beginning, men and women were made for each other: "And the LORD God said, It is not good that the man should be alone; I will make him an help meet for him" (Genesis 2:18 KJV). God has planted a desire within us to have a relationship not only with Him, but with a member of the opposite sex. The key word here is *opposite*. Because they are opposite, a man and a woman "complement each other. (*Complement*: to fill up or complete that which is required to supply a deficiency)."[51] That is not to say that one is more deficient than the other, or that one is above the other for "in the Lord, neither is woman independent of man, nor is man independent of woman" (1 Corinthians 11:11 NASB). No, the Lord made us equal, to complement each other, and to become as one.

Next we need to acknowledge that, as Richard J. Foster writes, "God desires that marriages be healthy, whole, and permanent."[52] In spite of our differences in background, personality, likes and dislikes, we need to become compatible. Larry Burkett writes, "If two people in a marriage are just alike one of them is unnecessary. In great part, God puts opposites together. . .so that one will offset the extremes of the other one. If we look at differences as a problem rather than as a balance, we will end up arguing a lot. By recognizing the differences as an asset, a couple can become one working unit. That is what God desires."[53]

Now that we know the plan and the innate problem, what's the procedure? It's relatively simple: Marriage takes work. And the more effort you give to "getting along together," the better and more rewarding your marriage will be. Part of this work "effort" requires you to *commit* to, *communicate* with, *compliment*, and *care* for each other.

When you and your spouse said, "I do," you promised to

love, honor, and cherish each other "until death do [you] part." That's quite a vow of commitment to make before family, friends, and God. And it is one you are meant to keep. The power of staunch commitment is an awesome thing when combined with the power of love.

Once committed, you need to communicate. Don't become so caught up in the world that you become two ships passing in the night, merely blaring your horns once in a while and then heading into separate seas. And when you do converse, watch your words and also *mean* what you say. Last Valentine's Day, I made it a point to tell my husband not to get me anything other than a card. He listened to me! I couldn't believe it. Not a single flower or piece of chocolate! Although I was sorely disappointed, the experience taught me I need to make sure I mean what I say.

Now that you're communicating, take the time to compliment each other. As the years progress, husbands and wives tend to get into a rut. Prevent your rut from becoming a chasm by "rejoic[ing] in the wife [or husband] of your youth" (Proverbs 5:18 NIV). When you work at praising and complimenting each other day after day, the flame of your love will burn ever greater and you'll find yourselves rejoicing in each other's presence.

But commitment, communication, and compliments will be hollow at best unless you care for each other using the power of the *love* described in 1 Corinthians 13:4–8. Make it a point to practice this love every day.

Pray for each other and fuel your marriage with the power of love so that you may "enjoy life with the [one] whom you love all the days of your fleeting life. . .for this is your reward" (Ecclesiastes 9:9 NASB*)*. And at night when the lights go out, take time to adore that special person God has made just for you.

Christ when I lie down.

Two in One

" 'A man will leave his father and mother and be united to his wife, and the two will
become one flesh'. . . . So they are no longer two, but one. Therefore
what God has joined together, let man not separate."
MATTHEW 19:5–6 NIV

*L*ord, my spouse and I are two who have been united into one. I praise You and thank You for leading me to my other half. He/She is more than I could ever have hoped for or dreamed. Bless our marriage, bless our union, bless our lives. Help us to grow closer together with each passing year. Lead us to do what You have called us to do, as one standing before You this day.

My Reward in Life

Enjoy life with the [one] whom you love all the days of your fleeting life which He has
given to you under the sun; for this is your reward in life.
ECCLESIASTES 9:9 NASB

*L*ife passes so quickly, Lord. Yet for this precious amount of time I have here on earth, I want to enjoy life with my spouse. He/she is so dear to me. Thank You for rewarding me with his/her presence in the morning as I wake and at night when the lights go out. Thank You for filling me with thoughts of my lover throughout the day. Bless my spouse this morning. Let Your love flow through me and into my other half.

Romance

Let him kiss me with the kisses of his mouth: for thy love is better than wine.
SONG OF SOLOMON 1:2 KJV

*I*t just keeps getting better and better, Lord. What an awesome love I share with my spouse! In the beginning of our union, our kisses were timid and shy. Now we are burning with a passion that at times is hard to quench. As the years go by, we grow deeper and deeper in love in every way. Thank You for my loving spouse. Thank You for completing me with his/her presence. Thank You for the romance in our lives.

Getting Stronger Every Day

For if what is passing away was glorious, what remains is much more glorious.
2 CORINTHIANS 3:11 NKJV

*L*ord, my spouse and I have been through such trials, yet each time we make it over a hurdle together, our love grows stronger. What we had in the beginning of our marriage was good, but what we have now is better. Continue to help us through the trials of this life. Help us to keep a united front before our children. And in all things, may we praise Your name for the wonders and joy of marital love.

Double Standards

Let love be without hypocrisy.
ROMANS 12:9 NKJV

*D*ear God, I can't believe it. I was so upset with my spouse because I thought he/she was taking me for granted. But it seems as if I have been doing the exact same thing. Lord, when everything was so new to our marriage, we spent so much more time together and did special things for each other, but in the passing of years, we seem to have fallen into a rut. Help us to treasure each other more, Lord, beginning this morning. Show me how I can let my spouse know he/she is more precious to me than silver or gold.

A Fresh Passion

Many waters cannot quench love, neither can the floods drown it.
SONG OF SOLOMON 8:7 KJV

I feel as if we are just going through the motions, Lord. Could it be that we have fallen out of love with each other? But that's not what marriage is all about, is it? There are times when it feels as if we have fallen out of love, but we still do care deeply for each other. Help us to remain patient. Help our love to bloom anew. Give us a fresh passion for each other. Light the flame of our desire, Lord. Keep us as one.

Wounded and Bleeding

This one thing I do, forgetting those things which are behind,
and reaching forth unto those things which are before.
PHILIPPIANS 3:13 KJV

*L*ord, help us to put our past troubles behind us and look forward to the days ahead. Help us to forget some of the things that we have done and said to each other. Our marriage is wounded and bleeding, Lord. We need Your balm of love to heal it. Give us Your special touch so that we may never part. For what You have brought together shall not be put asunder. Give us strength, hope, wisdom, and guidance.

The Spouse of Your Youth

May your fountain be blessed, and may you rejoice in the [spouse] of your youth.
PROVERBS 5:18 NIV

*M*y spouse and I are getting up there in years, Lord. We don't look, think, or act as young as we did on the day we said, "I do." But we feel so blessed. You have given us so much through this marriage. The love that we still feel for each other is all-consuming. We rejoice with each other in Your presence. May this union continue to be blessed by Your hand until "death do we part."

Making Love

"Come, let us drink our fill of love until morning; let us delight ourselves with caresses."
PROVERBS 7:18 NASB

*T*hank You, Lord, for the intimacy my spouse and I share. Thank You for the children that have come as a result of our union. They are truly our treasure. Continue to give us the desire for each other, for the times of passion and the times of cuddling. It is like heaven on earth. Bless my spouse this day. Give him/her the strength to meet the challenges ahead. Bring him/her home safely and into my loving arms.

Choosing Words Carefully

Do you see a man who is quick with his words?
There is more hope for a fool than for him.
PROVERBS 29:20 NLV

I did it again, Lord. I spoke before I thought and now I have wounded my spouse. According to Your Word, there is more hope for a fool than for me. I feel so terrible about what I said. I know I cannot take away the words I have spoken. All I can say is that I'm sorry. Forgive me, Father, for the words I spoke. My heart is so heavy within me. Give me the courage to ask my spouse for forgiveness. And may this rift in our union be speedily mended. Heal our marriage, Lord. Give me hope.

A Good Wife

A good wife. . .is worth far more than rubies that make one rich. The heart of her
husband trusts in her, and he will never stop getting good things.
She does him good and not bad all the days of her life.

PROVERBS 31:10–12 NLV

*L*ord, I have such a good wife! I know I can trust her. She always makes me feel like I am the center of her world, treasured, respected, and loved. I cannot praise her enough. Thank You for blessing me with her heart. Help me to protect her and be her spiritual leader. Give me the right words to tell her how much I love her and need her. Never let me take her for granted for that would truly be a sin. Thank You for allowing me to share her life and her heart while we live on this earth.

Anger Issues

If you are angry, do not let it become sin. Get over your anger before the day is finished.

EPHESIANS 4:26 NLV

I did it again, Lord. I went to bed angry with my spouse and spent a sleepless night because of it. I feel awful today. My spouse and I went our separate ways this morning with tension between us. Now we'll be brooding about it all day. Calm my anger, Lord. Forgive me for letting it go this long. Give us the right words to say to each other when we are alone again tonight. Help us heal this breach, to Your glory.

Record of Wrongs

*[Love] does not demand its own way. It is not irritable,
and it keeps no record of being wronged.*
1 CORINTHIANS 13:5 NLT

I can't seem to help myself, Lord. I have this list in my mind of all the things my spouse has done to hurt me. I cannot seem to let them go. And it is harming our marriage. Help me to give up on this record of wrongs. Give us a clean slate this morning and every morning. Help me not to keep on bringing up the past but to just have hope for tomorrow. May the power of love erase all these wrongs and give us back the magic of yesterday.

Undying Love

*Love never gives up, never loses faith, is always hopeful,
and endures through every circumstance.*
1 CORINTHIANS 13:7 NLT

*M*y love for my spouse will never die, Lord, because we believe in You. We know You have brought us together and will keep us together. We will never give up on this marriage, nor lose faith in each other, nor lose hope in our circumstances. We are in this until the end and, although we may not love every minute of it, we do love each other and You. And because of that, we are growing stronger every day. Thank You, Jesus, for the power of love!

My Family

The Power of Words

Everyone should be quick to listen, slow to speak and slow to become angry.

James 1:19 niv

*W*ords have power. We can use words to heal or harm, lift or lower, teach or taunt.

When you talk to your spouse, children, and parents, are your words building them up or tearing them down? Have you said things that you wished you could take back? As Frederick Buechner writes, "Words spoken in deep love or deep hate set things in motion within the human heart that can never be reversed."[54]

As parents, we have a profound influence on our children and much of that influence is communicated through our words. The great evangelist Billy Sunday once shared this story: "A man sent a friend of mine some crystals from the *Scientific American* and said: 'One of these crystals as small as a pinpoint will give a noticeable green hue to 7,000 gallons of water.' Think of it! Power enough in an atom to color 7,000 gallons of water. There is power in a word or act to adversely influence a boy and through him afflict a community. There is power enough in a word to color the life of that child so it will become a power to lift the world to Jesus Christ. The mother will put in motion influences that will either touch heaven or hell."

Our words can even color how a child thinks about himself.

Bill Gillham writes, "Verbalizing to a child that he is stupid, ugly, clumsy, uncoordinated, lazy. . .and so on gives him solid evidence that he really *is* a loser."[55] If a child is told he is lazy often enough, he will begin to think he is lazy. And eventually what he thinks he is, he will become for Proverbs 23:7 tells us that "as he thinks in his heart, so is he" (NKJV).

Our children are what they eat. What words are you feeding your family? Words poisoned with sarcasm, tainted with anger, and seasoned with insults? Or nourishing morsels laced with praise, colored with encouragement, and spiced with honor?

What steps can you take to ensure that you are feeding your family, your children, a healthy conversational diet? First, when communicating, *be quick to listen.* Larry Burkett writes, "How many times have you jumped into a conversation impulsively, to add your two cents, only to regret it later? Remember, 'He who gives an answer before he hears, it is folly and shame to him' (Proverbs 18:13)."[56]

Second, be *slow to speak.* Think and pray before you let any words come out of your mouth. Proverbs 16:1 says, "The plans of the mind and orderly thinking belong to man, but from the Lord comes the [wise] answer of the tongue" (Proverbs 16:1 AMP). Praying *before* speaking will save you a lot of heartache.

When you do speak, be *slow to become angry.* Keep a rein on your emotions by using "patient persistence [which] pierces through indifference; gentle speech [which] breaks down rigid defenses" (Proverbs 25:15 THE MESSAGE). If you yell and scream at your children, you will most likely raise ungodly daughters and sons that yell and scream at everyone else.

The words you use will influence the way your children view your faith. Larry Burkett writes: "Children are rarely attracted to a weak, watered-down version of Christianity that says one thing and does another. . . . You may be the only 'Gospel' that someone near you will 'read.' If unbelievers see hypocrisy in your life, they'll have no desire to be Christians."[57] What do your children "read" when you converse with them?

And if, after an intense discussion, you realize that in

spite of yourself you've said some things you shouldn't have, be humble enough to apologize. When you do, chances are good that your children will be more ready to apologize to you—and to others throughout life. If you "train up a child in the way he should go, even when he is old he will not depart from it" (Proverbs 22:6 NASB).

By the power of your godly words, you can equip your child with three faiths: "Faith in himself. . .that he can do anything which he wants to do if it is done with God's blessing and approval. . . . Faith in you and in all other children of God. . .by setting him the example you want him to follow. . . . Faith in God. . .that God loves him, that God cares for him, that God wants him to be happy."[58]

Ask God to help you gain control of your tongue. Use your words to build up your family members (see 1 Thessalonians 5:11). Honor others—those above (parents, grandparents), beside (spouses), and below you (children and grandchildren)—more than you honor yourself (see Philippians 2:3), by listening to them, praying before you speak, and responding in gentleness.

In conversation, take care not to "withhold good from those to whom it is due, when it is in the power of your hand to do so" (Proverbs 3:27 NKJV). When you sit down to talk with your children, listen and then pray for the right words to say in calmness of tone and manner, demonstrating that Christ is at the center of your speech and life.

Christ when I sit down.

Morning Prayer for Godly Words

The Sovereign LORD has given me his words of wisdom, so that I know how to comfort the weary. Morning by morning he wakens me and opens my understanding to his will.
ISAIAH 50:4 NLT

*L*ord, here I am this morning, awaiting Your words of wisdom. I need to have a talk with my child today and I don't know what to say or how to say it. Give me direction. Open my eyes, heart, and spirit to understanding Your will for me and my child. I want to know how to speak words to comfort, direct, and assist him/her. Help me, O Lord. Guide the words of my tongue.

Made a Mistake

Indeed, we all make many mistakes. For if we could control our tongues, we would be perfect and could also control ourselves in every other way.
JAMES 3:2 NLT

O God, if only I could control my tongue! My life is more like "Open mouth, insert foot." And that's just what I've done. Is there any way to remedy this situation? Help me in this endeavor. Give me the courage to be humble, to go to my child and admit I've made a mistake. May he/she forgive me as I have forgiven my child so often in the past, and how You constantly forgive all of us. Help us put this incident behind us. Give me the wisdom to do better next time. All to Your glory!

Curb My Tongue

The tongue can bring death or life; those who love to talk will reap the consequences.
PROVERBS 18:21 NLT

*L*ord, my tongue just went on and on—and now I am reaping the consequences. When will I ever learn when to stop talking? It seems I continually belabor a point until my child has zoned out and becomes unresponsive. Help me to weigh my words carefully, to say only what You want me to say. In other words, help me to zip up my mouth!

Jesus' Word Power

[Jesus said,] "The Spirit alone gives eternal life. Human effort accomplishes nothing. And the very words I have spoken to you are spirit and life."
JOHN 6:63 NLT

I try and try, but my efforts accomplish nothing when I have not come first to You in prayer. I need to do things in Your strength for otherwise I am useless. I need Your power behind me when I speak. I need Your strength. Allow Your Word to speak to me. Guide my way by Your gentle voice. May my spirit and Yours become one this day.

Kids' Trash Talk

There is a generation that curses its father, and does not bless its mother.
PROVERBS 30:11 NKJV

*L*ord, the things my kid is saying these days! I don't know how to handle this situation. My child's words are cutting to both me and his/her father. Give me the right words to say to curb this kind of trash talk. This baby that I once held in my arms is growing up and I want him/her to grow up in You, to know You, to love You, and to follow You. To do that I desperately need Your help. Give me the wisdom I need to guide my child to You through thought, word, and deed.

Honoring Others with My Mouth

Don't try to impress others. Be humble, thinking of others as better than yourselves.
PHILIPPIANS 2:3 NLT

I don't need fancy words to impress others. I only need words guided by the mind of Christ. Help me, Lord, to honor others with my speech. I want to lift people up, not bring them down. I want to bring joy to the hearts of others, not sorrow. Give me a better attitude, positive words, and encouraging remarks. Guard my mouth and, when necessary, put Your hand upon it to keep it shut.

Need to Discipline

*Discipline your children, and they will give you peace of mind
and will make your heart glad.*
PROVERBS 29:17 NLT

*D*isciplining is easier said than done. It's true—it seems to hurt me more than it does my child. Is that how it is when You discipline me? That's something to think about. I'm sorry, Lord, for all the grief I have caused You. That makes it easier for me to pardon the grief my child causes me. Give me the right words I need to discipline my child today. Give me peace of mind so that both my heart and (eventually) his/hers are glad!

Kind Versus Cutting Words

Kind words heal and help; cutting words wound and maim.
PROVERBS 15:14 THE MESSAGE

*W*ords have cut me to the quick. Now I know how others feel when I harm them with my words. It really hurts. I feel very wounded. My stomach is filled with anger, sorrow, embarrassment, bitterness, and rage. Lord, give me a kind thought from Your Word today, scripture that will heal and build me back up. Take this sorrow from me and replace it with a spirit of forgiveness. Lift me up to Your rock of refuge.

Building Up

Encourage (admonish, exhort) one another and edify (strengthen and build up) one another.

1 THESSALONIANS 5:11 AMP

*O*kay, Lord, today not one negative thought is going to go through my head and come of out my mouth. This morning I will drench myself in Your Word and come out smiling. I want to spread to others the joy You plant in my heart. Give me the right words to say at the right moment to build up others. Give me words of praise, words of wisdom, and words of encouragement.

Living My Faith

If you claim to be religious but don't control your tongue, you are fooling yourself, and your religion is worthless.

JAMES 1:26 NLT

*L*ord, I want to live my faith before my children and others. To do that I need to be able to control my words, but sometimes, although I know this is impossible, my tongue seems to have a "mind" of its own. Help me rein in my mouth. Give me words that will lead my children to You. Help me to live a life that is rich in Your love—and may that love affect my speech. Begin with me this morning and show me how to live this faith.

Three Steps to Good Speech

Everyone should be quick to listen, slow to speak and slow to become angry.
JAMES 1:19 NIV

*H*elp me with all these steps, Lord. Step number one: I need to work on my listening skills. Too often I find myself thinking of a response instead of listening to what my child is saying, and then I am rushing in with a comment or advice before he's/ she's even stopped talking. Help me to sit, listen, and wait. Step number two: Remind me to pray before I speak. I need to be patient, not letting my mouth run ahead of You. And step number three: Take away my anger. That is not of You. Calm my spirit. Give me a cool head, Your thoughts, and wise words.

Needing a Tender Heart

Let all bitterness, wrath, anger, clamor, and evil speaking be put away from you, with all malice. And be kind to one another, tenderhearted, forgiving one another, even as God in Christ forgave you.
EPHESIANS 4:31–32 NKJV

*T*ake away all the bitterness I feel today, and with it the anger and words I want to say but know I shouldn't. Help me not to avenge my honor with evil words. Give me Your tender heart. Help me to forgive the one who has hurt me, just as You, Lord, forgave me. Make this a new morning. Wipe the slate clean. I want to live as You did, Lord, with gentle words, a peaceful spirit, and a loving heart.

Keep My Tongue from Evil

*For let him who wants to enjoy life and see good days [good—whether apparent or not]
keep his tongue free from evil and his lips from guile (treachery, deceit).*

1 PETER 3:10 AMP

I want to enjoy life! I want to see good days! But to do that, I need to keep my tongue from evil and my lips—my eternally flapping lips—from negative words, lies, and malice. There is no way I can do this by myself. No, I need Your Spirit to fill me with love and peace and joy. I need Your hand to guide me. I need Your mind to dwell within me. Give me the strength, grace, and peace I need to speak to others today.

The Good Words

*Then was our mouth filled with laughter, and our tongue with singing: then said they
among the heathen, the LORD hath done great things for them.*

PSALM 126:2 KJV

*Y*ou have filled my mouth with laughter! My tongue is singing Your praises! Others see me and say, "Wow! Look at what the Lord has done for her!" I am so alive in You this morning. And it is because I am not only praying and reading Your Word, but I am allowing You to live in me and am putting Your Word into action. It can't get any better than this, and it's all because of Your sacrifice, Your dying for me. Thank You, Jesus, for making me whole and happy in You!

My Challenges

The Power of Faith-Based Boldness

*When we trust in him, we're free to say whatever needs to be said,
bold to go wherever we need to go.*
EPHESIANS 3:11 THE MESSAGE

*R*emember the *Star Trek* series? At the beginning of every episode, we'd hear Captain Kirk saying, "Space, the final frontier. These are the voyages of the starship *Enterprise*. Its five-year mission: To explore strange new worlds. To seek out new life and new civilizations. To boldly go where no man has gone before."

Okay, we're not starships, but each of our lives is uniquely different, and we often encounter situations where "no man has gone before." But how can we learn to face each new "enterprise" boldly? We can start by modeling the kind of faith-based boldness that David exhibited during his encounter with Goliath (see 1 Samuel 17).

The youngest of Jesse's sons, David spent many hours in the fields, taking care of his father's sheep. It was here that David prayed and meditated on God. His reliance on God was evidence of the intimate relationship David had developed with God at an early age. This intimacy with the Lord allowed David's faith to grow. David knew God would be with him in every situation. It was his faith that gave him the boldness to do whatever God called him to do.

When David left his father's fields to check on his brothers who were with King Saul's army, it was not by chance that his visit coincided with the nine-foot-nine-inch-tall Philistine warrior named Goliath, who was defying the army of Israel. As David began talking to the soldiers, he encountered his first challenge in the form of his oldest brother Eliab, who said: "Why have you come down? And with whom have you left those few sheep in the wilderness? I know your insolence and the wickedness of your heart; for you have come down in order to see the battle" (1 Samuel 17:28 NASB).

Now David *could* have taken this attack upon his character to heart. John Maxwell writes, "Many negative seeds are planted in our minds until we often stop short of what we can do for God, for others, and for ourselves."[59] But because of his faith-based boldness, David did not allow Eliab's negative comments to take root in his mind. He was able to simply turn away and continue on his mission.

David's next confrontation was with King Saul, who "from his shoulders upward. . .was taller than any of the [other children of Israel]" (1 Samuel 9:2 NKJV). Now, you'd think that because of his size Saul himself would have fought Goliath. Instead, Saul tried to discourage the only one willing to face the giant. Saul said to David: "There's no way you can fight this Philistine and possibly win! You're only a boy, and he's been a man of war since his youth" (1 Samuel 17:33 NLT).

Saul was right. Although David had always managed to keep his lambs safe, he had no battlefield experience. But inexperience can be a good thing. Tim Elmore writes, "When we are inexperienced, we tend to lean on God for results. We recognize how little we possess—and how much we need His help."[60] David had always relied on God to deliver him and he wasn't about to stop doing so now—nor was he going to allow

Saul to dampen his enthusiasm. Instead, he boldly responded to his king: "I've been a shepherd, tending sheep for my father. Whenever a lion or bear came and took a lamb from the flock, I'd go after it, knock it down, and rescue the lamb. . . . GOD, who delivered me from the teeth of the lion and the claws of the bear, will deliver me from this Philistine" (1 Samuel 17:34–37 THE MESSAGE).

John Maxwell writes, "A successful person is one who takes the cold water dumped on his plans, heats it with his enthusiasm, and manufactures the steam, to push ahead."[61] Our David was so successful in refuting Saul's discouraging remarks that the king himself became enthusiastic and said to him, "Go! And may God help you."

Goliath took one look at this lowly shepherd boy and began to taunt him. David responded to such intimidation by declaring that he came in the name of God, that he depended upon God for success, and that this success would all be to God's glory! Then David actually "*hurried and ran* toward the army to meet the Philistine" (1 Samuel 17:48 NKJV, emphasis added). What boldness!

Unlike Saul and Eliab, David was able "to boldly go where no man has gone before." Because of his intimate knowledge of God, David was able to turn away from a maligner, defend himself before a discourager, and fell a giant intimidator with one smooth stone. By using faith-based boldness, David met the challenges presented to him and, as a result, routed the entire Philistine army. All for God's glory!

If we build up our confidence by spending time in the Word, prayer, and meditation, getting to know our God intimately, we can be like David, who, with faith-based boldness, "rose early in the morning" (1 Samuel 17:20 NKJV) to meet every challenge God put in his path.

Christ when I arise.

Dissuaded from Your Goal

They were just trying to intimidate us, imagining that they could discourage us and stop the work. So I continued the work with even greater determination.
NEHEMIAH 6:9 NLT

*L*ord, here I am trying to take on this work and others are trying to intimidate me, telling me there is no way I can meet the challenge You have set before me. But I have faith in You. I know that with You in my life, I can do whatever You call me to do. Help me not to let others dissuade me from my goal. Give me the faith that David sought from You, the kind that does not waver but goes boldly forward.

Bold and Diligent

"Be bold and diligent. And GOD *be with you as you do your best."*
2 CHRONICLES 19:11 THE MESSAGE

I'm working as hard as I can to meet my challenge. I want to do my best, knowing that You are with me all the way. Help me to be brave. Help me not to panic. Neither fear nor anxiety is of You. I need to focus on You, to build up my faith and my confidence. Help me not to deviate from my course. I am here this morning, ready to listen to Your voice. Lead me, gentle Shepherd, where You want me to go.

Facing the Unknown

"And now, compelled by the Spirit, I am going to Jerusalem,
not knowing what will happen to me there."
ACTS 20:22 NIV

O Lord, I feel called to take on this new challenge. I can feel the Spirit drawing me into this latest endeavor. But I don't know what's going to happen. Oh, how I sometimes wish I could see into the future. Lord, help me to have confidence, trust, and faith in Your will for my life. Help me to just put one foot in front of the other, to do the next thing, to continue walking in Your way. And when I get there, I will give You all the glory!

Fearlessness

Though an army may encamp against me, my heart shall not fear.
PSALM 27:3 NKJV

I remember the story of David, how he faced opposition from his brother, his king, and then a huge giant, all under the watchful eye of his enemies. But he was not afraid. Oh, that I would have such faith. Sometimes I get so scared my heart begins beating a mile a minute. And those are the times when I have taken my eyes off of You. Keep my focus on Your Word. Plant this verse in my heart so that when dread comes upon me, I can say these words and kiss fear good-bye.

Standing with God

Everyone deserted me. May it not be held against them. But the Lord stood at my side and gave me strength. . . . And I was delivered.

2 TIMOTHY 4:16–17 NIV

*A*ll of a sudden, I am as alone as David when he stood before Goliath. But I am not going to be mad at others for deserting me. I don't need them. All I need is You. You are my Lord, my Savior, my Deliverer, my Rock, my Refuge. You are by my side. I can feel Your presence right here, right now. Oh, how wonderful You are! Thank You for giving me the power I need. Thank You for never leaving me.

Support of Fellow Believers

When [Paul] would not be dissuaded, we gave up and said, "The Lord's will be done."

ACTS 21:14 NIV

*S*ometimes those who don't know You think that believers like me are crazy. But we're not. We just know that when You call us to do something, when You put a challenge before us, we are to go forward with no fear. We are bold in You, Lord! How awesome is that! And thankfully, fellow believers encourage us, knowing that if it is Your will, all will be well. What would I do without that support? Thank You for planting my feet in a nice broad place, surrounded by fellow believers who love and pray for me.

Our Help

Our help is in the name of the LORD, who made heaven and earth.
PSALM 124:8 NKJV

I need look no further than You, Lord, to help me. It is Your name that I trust. It is Your power that will help me meet this challenge. After all, You made me. You know the plan for my life. You have equipped me to do what You have called me to do. Help me not to rely on myself but on You and Your power. That is what is going to give me victory in this life. Thank You for hearing and answering my prayer.

My Armor

I will not trust in my bow, nor shall my sword save me. But You have saved us from our enemies, and have put to shame those who hated us. In God we boast all day long, and praise Your name forever.
PSALM 44:6–8 NKJV

I do not trust in my talents, diligence, money, education, luck, or others to help me meet this challenge. I trust in You. My power is in the faith-based boldness that only comes from knowing You intimately. With that weapon in my arsenal, there is only victory ahead. Those who say I cannot do what You have called me to do will be put to shame. But that's not why I continue to meet this challenge. I go forward because I want to bring glory to You. It is in You that I boast all day long. I praise Your name, my Strength and my Deliverer.

Hope

"And now, Lord, what do I wait for? My hope is in You."
PSALM 39:7 NKJV

Some hope in employers or money or connections or that one big break. I hope in You and what You want to do through me while I'm here on earth. Don't let me drag my feet in fear but boldly run forward as David did when he faced Goliath. David knew You, and he knew that You would always be with him, no matter what. That's a fabulous faith. Empower me with that today so that I, like David, can go out with You and take on giants.

Make Me Bold

On the day I called, You answered me; You made me bold with strength in my soul.
PSALM 138:3 NASB

Sometimes I feel like a ninety-five-pound weakling when it comes to my faith. I let my doubts and fears overtake me and then find myself shrinking from the challenges You put before me. Lord, I ask You to make me bold. Give me the strength to take on all comers. To do what You want me to do. Dispel the darkness that surrounds me. Bring me to where You want me to be. Give me strength in my soul!

By Faith, I Go

By faith Abraham, when he was called, obeyed by going out to a place which he was to receive for an inheritance; and he went out, not knowing where he was going.

HEBREWS 11:8 NASB

*I*n these days of online directional services and personal navigation systems, I can't imagine not knowing where I am going. What Abraham might have given for a map! But that's what faith is all about, isn't it? It's the substance of things hoped for, the evidence of things unseen. Give me that faith, Lord, as I take on this challenge. I don't know where it will lead or how it will all turn out, but by faith I will obey Your call. I will go out, not knowing, because I trust in You!

At the Throne

So let us come boldly to the throne of our gracious God. There we will receive his mercy, and we will find grace to help us when we need it most.

HEBREWS 4:16 NLT

*H*ere I am again, Lord, coming boldly before You, kneeling at the foot of Your throne. I need Your mercy this morning, and although it seems like I ask for this over and over again, give me more faith, Lord. Help me not to run from this challenge. Give me the grace, strength, energy, talent, and intelligence that I need to make this come out right. I come to You, bowing down, asking for Your love and power to fill me and to give me the strength I need to accomplish the challenges before me this day.

God Looks at the Heart

But the LORD said to Samuel, "Do not consider his appearance or his height, for I have rejected him. The LORD does not look at the things man looks at. Man looks at the outward appearance, but the LORD looks at the heart."

1 SAMUEL 16:7 NIV

*S*ome people look at me and say, "There's no way you can do this." But with You I can do anything, Lord. You don't just look at my appearance. When You look at me, You look directly at my heart. I know that You have made me to use my particular talents to accomplish particular tasks here on earth. You know my purpose, my path. Help me use all my resources to meet this challenge before me. All to Your glory!

In God's Strength

I have strength for all things in Christ Who empowers me [I am ready for anything and equal to anything through Him Who infuses inner strength into me; I am self-sufficient in Christ's sufficiency].

PHILIPPIANS 4:13 AMP

*I*t's amazing—I can do all things through You! You give me the power! You give me the energy! You give me the ways and the means! As I lie here, in Your presence, I feel all the energy emanating from You. Oh, what a feeling! Give me that strength I need to accomplish the goals You set before me. Plant the words, "I can do all things through God—He strengthens me!" in my heart forever and ever.

Conclusion

Prayer has the power to heal the sick, feed the hungry, protect the endangered, replenish the weary, mend the heart, save the soul, strengthen the spirit, transform a life, and change the world. Prayer makes the impossible possible.

Believe in this power. Bolster your faith by delving into God's Word and examining the records of His people. There you will find that by prayer, Jehoshaphat and the citizens of Judah and Jerusalem were miraculously saved from their enemies (see 2 Chronicles 20); Joshua and his army brought down the walls of Jericho (see Joshua 6); Elijah had the power to bring fire down from heaven (see 1 Kings 18:38; 2 Kings 1:10–12); raise a widow's son from the dead (see 1 Kings 17:17–24) and divide a river (see 2 Kings 2:7–8); and the apostles were able to heal the sick, walk through prison doors, and exorcise demons.

This amazing authority, this power that can transform your life, is also available to you. R. A. Torrey writes, "Prayer has as much power today. . .as it has ever had. God has not changed; and His ear is just as quick to hear the voice of real prayer, and His hand is just as long and strong to save, as it ever was"[62] (see Isaiah 59:1).

Every morning when you arise you have the opportunity to come to your Lord and Savior and take hold of the power of prayer. Run to His presence. He is waiting for you to seek His face, to ask Him whatever your heart desires.

James 4:2 says, "You do not have, because you do not ask God" (NIV). Are you asking? Do you keep on asking? George

Müller said, "The great fault of the children of God is, they do not continue in prayer: they do not go on praying; they do not persevere. If they desire anything for God's glory, they should pray until they get it."[63] If you and I fail to be persistent in prayer, how will we ever receive "immeasurably more than all we ask or imagine, according to his power that is at work within us" (Ephesians 3:20 NIV)?

David Jeremiah writes, "What we do for the Lord is entirely dependent upon what we receive from the Lord, and what we receive from the Lord is entirely dependent upon what we are in the Lord, and what we are in the Lord is entirely dependent upon the time we spend alone with the Lord in prayer."[64]

Don't let the fast pace of this world keep you from experiencing the power of prayer. Bill Hybels writes, "Prayerless people cut themselves off from God's prevailing power, and the frequent result is the familiar feeling of being overwhelmed, overrun, beaten down, pushed around, defeated. Surprising numbers of people are willing to settle for lives like that. Don't be one of them. Nobody has to live like that. *Prayer is the key to unlocking God's prevailing power in your life.*"[65]

Approach God, knowing that He is with you, that if you ask anything in Jesus' name, He will do it (see John 14:14). R. A. Torrey writes, "Prayer is the key that unlocks all the storehouses of God's infinite grace and power. All that God is, and all that God has, is at the disposal of prayer. But we must use the key. *Prayer can do anything that God can do, and as God can do anything, prayer is omnipotent.* No one can stand against the man who. . .really prays."[66] Take hold of the key of prayer to open the doors of your life in Christ.

When we arise each morning, we have the privilege of coming to Christ in faith and entering into His presence in prayer. He is "as a *door open* for passage and communication,"[67] our gateway to God the Father. He speaks to us when we listen to His voice and read His Word. Outside of our prayer time, He speaks to us by the answers to our petitions, by the circumstances in our lives, and through other people (via sermons, writings, music, conversation, and so on). But if we use prayer to open the door and then just leave our petitions, not lingering to listen, how can we hone in to the messages He is ready to impart? How can we be sure to "catch" His communiqués?

One method we can use to retain God's personal messages to us is by keeping a spiritual journal. When we approach the throne with pen and paper in hand, ready to record the sorrows, circumstances, obstacles, and blessings in our lives, we are prone to examine our inner self more closely and, in turn, give more power to heartfelt prayers.

The Bible contains several examples of spiritual journaling. Numbers 33:2 tells us that "at the LORD's direction, Moses kept a written record of their progress" (NLT). Donald S. Whitney writes, "Many psalms are records of David's personal spiritual journey with the Lord."[68] Ecclesiastes is a record of those things Solomon "perceived" (Ecclesiastes 2:14 KJV) or "said in [his] heart" (Ecclesiastes 2:1, 15; 3:17–18 KJV). Lamentations is Jeremiah's revelation of the sorrow he felt in his heart for his people. And, like all the other Gospel accounts, the book of Luke is a journal-like record, with the book of Acts being a continuation of that "former account" (Acts 1:1 NKJV).

Follow the example of these great leaders of faith. Create your own spiritual journal to discern where God is leading you, to discover the patterns God is weaving into your days, to enhance the power and meaning of your prayers. With a daily record of how God helps you and interacts with you, you will receive encouragement, enabling you to trust Him more during the bleak times. A spiritual journal can also be a wonderful tool for future generations, to show them how God has worked in and through your life (see Psalm 102:18).

Use your journal to write down the Bible verses that most speak to your heart. Meditate on them, asking God to open your eyes to His meaning. Write out the gifts God has given you and ask Him for an opportunity to use them to His glory. List the ways you are thankful or needful, stressed or blessed. Use your journal to record your praises, prayer requests from other people, sermon notes or insights from books you're reading, or your personal petitions and answers to your prayers.

For examples of how to journal your prayers, you need only look to David's psalms. These wonderfully heartfelt prayers are filled with David's anguish for his present condition and current grievances, reminders to himself of how God has worked in his life, pleas for deliverance, lists of God's attributes, praises, thanksgiving, and the wonders of the world, insights into God's leading, and so on. Find those that speak to your heart, copy them into your journal, and make them your own prayers to God.

Approach your quiet time with an eager, open heart, knowing that prayer is the key to your life in Christ. In the early morning silence, allow the Holy Spirit to lead you to God's kingdom. As you spend time in His presence, growing closer to your Lord and Savior, you will become more like Him, filled with His light and love. Then when you rise from those moments in His presence, you will find yourself radiating His love to those around you.

As you grow in God's grace, may your spirit be so transformed that those you meet will be assured they have experienced a glimpse of Christ.

Christ in the heart of every [one] who thinks of me, Christ in the mouth of every one who speaks of me, Christ in the eye of every one that sees me, Christ in every ear that hears me.

Notes

1. E. M. Bounds, *The Complete Works of E. M. Bounds on Prayer* (Grand Rapids: Baker, 2004), 464.

2. Matthew Henry, *Matthew Henry's Commentary* (Grand Rapids: Zondervan, 1961), 89.

3. Text of the "Breastplate of St. Patrick" or "The Deer's Cry" obtained from Catholic Culture Document Library at www.catholicculture.org/docs/doc_view. cfm? recnum=139; © Copyright Trinity Communications 2006. All rights reserved.

4. David Jeremiah, *Prayer: The Great Adventure* (Sisters, Ore.: Multnomah, 1997), 75–76.

5. Rachel Hickson, *Supernatural Communication: The Privilege of Prayer* (Grand Rapids: Chosen, 2006), 28–29.

6. Neil T. Anderson, *Praying by the Power of the Spirit* (Eugene, Ore.: Harvest House Publishers, 2003), 38–39.

7. Bounds, 20.

8. Henry, 1277.

9. Ibid.

10. John Ayto, *Dictionary of Word Origins* (New York: Arcade Publishing, 1990), 374.

11. Dick Eastman and Jack Hayford, *Living and Praying in Jesus' Name* (Wheaton, Ill.: Tyndale House, 1988), 177.

12. John Maxwell, *Think on These Things* (Kansas City: Beacon Hill Press, 1979), 96.

13. Becky Tirabassi, *The Burning Heart Contract* (Brentwood, Tenn.: Integrity, 2005), 46.

14. Oswald Chambers, *My Utmost for His Highest* (Uhrichsville, Ohio: Barbour Publishing, 2000), December 31.

15. Andrew Murray, *Andrew Murray on Prayer* (New Kensington, Penn.: Whitaker House, 1998), 357.

16. Ibid., 217.

17. Richard J. Foster, *Celebration of Discipline* (New York: HarperCollins, 1998), 168.

18. Henrietta C. Mears, *What the Bible Is All About* (New York: HarperCollins, 1998), 198–199.

19. Walt Harrah, "Think About His Love," Integrity's Hosanna! Music, 1987.

20. Bill Gillham, *Lifetime Guarantee* (Eugene, Ore.: Harvest House, 1993), 92.

21. John Hull and Tim Elmore, *Pivotal Praying* (Nashville: Thomas Nelson, 2002), 44–45.

22. Bounds, 116.

23. Murray, 355.

24. Rick Warren, *The Purpose-Driven Life* (Grand Rapids: Zondervan, 2002), 227.

25. David J. Smith, *How Can I Ask God for Physical Healing?* (Grand Rapids: Chosen Books, 2005), 183.

26. Helmut Thielicke, *Encounter with Spurgeon* (Cambridge, England: James Clarke & Co., Ltd., 1978), ix.

27. C. S. Lewis, *The Joyful Christian* (New York: Macmillan Publishing Company, 1977), 210.

28. Hull and Elmore, 102.

29. Phillip Keller, *A Shepherd Looks at Psalm 23* (Grand Rapids: Zondervan, 1970), 83.

30. Oswald Chambers, *Daily Thoughts for Disciples* (Uhrichsville, Ohio: Barbour Publishing, 2005), January 9.

31. Keller, 82–83.

32. Ibid., 83.

33. Bill Hybels, *Too Busy Not to Pray* (Downers Grove, Ill: InterVarsity Press, 1988), 100.

34. Gordon MacDonald, *Ordering Your Private World* (Nashville: Thomas Nelson, 2003), 210–211.

35. Murray, 175.

36. Donald S. Whitney, *Spiritual Disciplines for the Christian Life* (Colorado Springs: NavPress, 1991), 135.

37. Henry, 315.

38. Larry Burkett, *Great Is Thy Faithfulness* (Uhrichsville, Ohio: Barbour Publishing, 1998), February 6.

39. Hull and Elmore, 190.

40. MacDonald, 30.

41. Burkett, May 5.

42. Ibid., January 30.

43. Frederick Buechner, *Listening to Your Life* (New York, HarperCollins, 1992), 54.

44. Burkett, August 28.

45. Jeremiah, 145.

46. Chambers, *Daily Thoughts for Disciples*, January 30.

47. Ibid., October 18.

48. *The Palm Beach Story*, Preston Sturges, 1942 Paramount Pictures, Inc., renewed 1969 by EMKA.

49. Lewis, 200.

50. Burkett, May 10.

51. Anabel Gillham, *The Confident Woman* (Eugene, Ore.: Harvest House Publishers, 1993), 172.

52. Foster, 43.

53. Burkett, June 15.

54. Buechner, 238.

55. Bill Gillham, 40.

56. Burkett, August 25.

57. Ibid., March 11.

58. Life Study Fellowship, *With God All Things Are Possible* (New York: Bantam Books, 1972), 58, 60–61.

59. Maxwell, 41.

60. Hull and Elmore, 158.

61. Maxwell, 41.

62. R. A. Torrey, *The Power of Prayer* (Grand Rapids: Zondervan, 1971), 17.

63. Roger Steer, *George Müller: Delighted in God!* (Wheaton, Ill.: Harold Shaw, 1975), 310.

64. Jeremiah, 41.

65. Hybels, 13.

66. Torrey, 17.

67. Henry, 1563.

68. Whitney, 196.

Other Power Prayers Titles

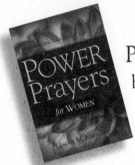

Power Prayers for Women
by Jackie M. Johnson

ISBN 978-1-59789-670-2

Power Prayers for Men
by John Hudson Tiner

ISBN 978-1-59789-858-4

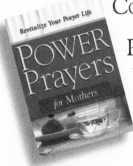

COMING MARCH 2008

Power Prayers for Mothers
by Rachel Quillin

ISBN 978-1-59789-998-7